got coach?

A coach's guide for being a top wholesaler

Michael Balch

How to leap frog the competition
and be the best wholesaler you can be.

iUniverse, Inc.
New York   Bloomington

iUniverse books may be ordered through booksellers or by contacting:

iUniverse
1663 Liberty Drive
Bloomington, IN 47403
www.iuniverse.com
1-800-Authors (1-800-288-4677)

ISBN: 978-1-4401-5057-9 (sc)
ISBN: 978-1-4401-5058-6 (ebook)

Printed in the United States of America

iUniverse rev. date: 07/15/2009

Contents

Introduction

Over the years I have witnessed a deterioration of the wholesaler and their skill level. When I first got into the business the wholesaler was much more of an entrepreneur than they are today. Today's wholesalers are more of a cookie cutter variety. They are smarter, better educated and better looking, but don't have the entrepreneurial spirit. There are also many more wholesalers in each market today. Advisors often joke about how they can spot a wholesaler from a mile away.

Because there is so much money in the marketplace and the majority of the wholesalers are not separating themselves from the pack it has convinced me to give something back to the business that I love. I started a training business, Good | Better | Best Inc. designed to coach wholesalers to be better than the competition. I believe that a well trained wholesaler can make an enormous amount of money for their firm and themselves.

I believe that wholesaling is one of the greatest occupations in the world. I have always loved wholesaling. I am not sure how I became a wholesaler. I cannot remember wholesaling being a choice on career day at college. Somewhere, somehow I became a wholesaler and am very happy about the outcome.

I have been in the distribution business as a wholesaler, a wire house specialist, national accounts manager and national sales manager for twenty-five years. I have seen numerous wholesalers come and go over the years. Over those twenty-five years I have compiled endless stories. I have seen so much in my wholesaling day that I decided to write a book about the do's and don'ts of wholesaling. I had originally thought about writing a book about all the funny and interesting people I have met over the years. While it would certainly be humorous, I do not imagine there would be much use for that kind of book. What I thought would be useful would be a book that all wholesalers could use to help their business.

During my many years (and firms) in the business I was a top wholesaler. I was a top wholesaler at top ten mutual fund companies (based on asset size), up-and-comers and start-ups. I have wholesaled through the best and worst of markets. I have covered stockbrokers, registered reps, account managers, financial consultants, and financial advisors, etc. I have pushed products, used modern portfolio theory, and studied for my CIMA, etc. I have covered wire houses, regionals, financial planners, banks, and insurance advisors, etc. I have also covered small, medium and large sized territories. I have wholesaled in every state except Alaska. There is not much I have not done.

Regardless of the market, product, channel or territory, I always adapted. It was the constant change in the business that I found exciting. Where else can you find a job that is always changing? Every time the business, as we knew it, changed, many firms and wholesalers changed accordingly. The ones who adapted to the change thrived, and the ones that didn't departed. Every time there was a change I learned a little bit more about our business.

Many of the main tenets of wholesaling remain the same, but the quality of wholesaling has diminished over the years. Not only have I seen a drop in the quality of wholesaling, but the advisors have as well. Over the years the wholesalers have gone from being invaluable partners to necessary nuisances. This became very clear four years ago when I took a position as a specialist at Merrill Lynch. In being a specialist I worked with hundreds of wholesalers. I was flabbergasted with how poor their skill levels were. I also had a chance to get an unedited view of the wholesalers from the advisors. Those comments were anything but complimentary of the wholesaling industry. It was at that point I decided when the time was right I would start a business of "coaching" wholesalers. I figured that I had profited from the weaker competition. I could have continued to profit from the disintegration of the wholesaler's skill level. However, it always bothered me that advisors that had not met me would lump me into the wide net of "another annoying wholesaler." It became clear that I would feel better profiting from improving the profession that I love.

In the world of wholesaling, we frequently get engulfed with everything going on around us. There are so many advisors at so many diverse firms and in multiple channels. You have numerous products and platforms. You are constantly besieged with value added marketing that headquarters' desires you to present. The market is up, the market is down, the market is volatile, or the market is flat. There are no new assets; there are trillions of dollars sitting on the sidelines. The office will not allow me in. The office does not allow walk-throughs. The office has a select list of firms allowed in. The office wants monetary support to get access. Nobody comes to lunch meetings. Only rookies come to lunch. I cannot get into see to top producers. The advisors sucked my time and are not doing any business.

My manager wants me to meet 40 advisors a day. My manager wants me to visit four offices a day. My manager wants to sell more Fixed Income. My manager requires me to use (named the sales method) in every meeting. My manager wishes to know why I am not visiting Advisor X. My manager wants to know why I am visiting Advisor Y so often. The list for opportunities and objections will continue to grow forever.

These are some of the many issues we deal with daily. Throughout the book I will pass on some of my knowledge and experiences in wholesaling. It doesn't matter what your wholesaling experiences may be or how many years you have wholesaled. It doesn't matter what channel you cover or where/what your territory looks like. This book will offer you some great new ideas and/or reassure you that what you are doing is correct.

It's a Numbers Game

The wholesaling landscape changes almost daily. When I first started wholesaling, it was strictly a numbers game. I was told that if you saw 100 people a week, you would be successful. If you saw 150 people a week you would be #1. That sounded easy enough, but the reality of 20-30 meetings per day was physically impossible. I wanted to be the top wholesaler so I tried to figure out how to see 150 people in a week.

It was clear that the best way for me to achieve those numbers would be to do lunch meetings. I set out to reach my goal. I set up five lunches per week, but I was averaging 5-6 "brokers" per meeting. That was not working either. Now I was seeing about 60 advisors per week. That seemed to be in line with what other wholesalers were seeing. I was still stuck on the 150 advisors per week number.

In my mind, the lunch meeting path was the way to hit my numbers. I set a strategy of only doing lunch meetings in large offices, and being the best presenter in my territory. I learned what advisors thought of the other wholesalers lunch meetings. I found out what the other wholesalers were doing well and what they were doing poorly. I then asked advisors what it would take for them to attend a wholesaler lunch meeting.

Once I had a good idea of what was going to get advisors in the lunch meetings, I went to the local University, Northwestern University, and hired a tutor to help me deliver an entertaining and informative presentation. I practice and practiced my presentations.

Once I was prepared, I delivered my presentation to all my large offices in my territory. After my first rotation, my numbers were slightly higher. That was only because I was in larger offices. The next rotation of presentations was better. More advisors were attending my lunch. There were new faces that I had not seen before. The third rotation through was a huge jump. The word had gotten out that my lunch meetings were worth attending. Eventually my presentations got better and better. I was considered the "King of the Lunch Meetings." I blew through the 150 advisors per week number and was sky rocketing to #1. The strategy worked and I spent my entire career as a top producer wherever I went.

What I learned back then, which still rings true today, is that it is *still* a numbers game. The more people you see, the better results you will achieve. It is your responsibility to control activity.

I will discuss in a later chapter how to maximize and gain appointments. In the next few chapters I am going to discuss the importance of "identifying your clients" and "where I can dominate." Remember my story of how to see 150 advisors per week. I identified my clients as those in large offices. I then dominated the competition by perfecting my presentation skills and becoming the "King of the Lunch Meeting." Throughout my entire wholesaling career, I was usually the first call to do a seminar.

Learn Where You Perform Best.

Sometimes we spend so much time running around like a chicken with their head cut off that we forget to stop and analyze what we are doing. Even though we are being active, we need to be more intelligent about who we visit. I once had a National Sales Manager that would say "work smarter, not harder." I might modify that to "work harder and smarter." What he really wanted us to do was to be smart about how we went about our business.

One of the things we all need to do is better understand our clientele and ourselves. If we can understand our strengths and weaknesses then we can better understand where and how we need to direct our efforts. Why not participate with similar advisors or platforms where I have a history of success. The best way to do this is to ask yourself a variety of questions that will help you understand your strengths.

Ask yourself these questions;

Do you do better in a particular firm? Is there a geographic location where you play better? Is a large part of your production coming from a certain platform such as, Mutual Funds, Annuities, SMA, UMA, 401K, 403B, etc.? Do you have greater success with teams or sole proprietors? Do your advisors make their own investment decisions or do they follow their firm's analyst or a market letter?

You will probably discover that there are certain advisors, in certain geographic locations, in certain platforms, that run their practice a similar way, and make their investment decisions in a similar method. If you can segment your clients in groups of strengths and then duplicate them your chance for success will go through the roof. Over the years, I found out I dominated in large suburban offices. I don't know why, but I was not going to fight the flow. I turned more attention to similar offices and my production went through the roof. I also had a lot of success with Latin advisors. I later asked why they did so much business with me. They said that I had no problem greeting them with a hug instead of a handshake. They said most Americans protect their "personal bubble" and keep people at a hand shake distance. They were comfortable with me. Being married to a Greek woman must have made me warm and fuzzy. It sounded crazy, but why fight it? I later found a great niche with these advisors and it became a great source of production for many years. If you have a natural strength, as crazy as it may be, KNOW IT… OWN IT… DOMINATE I

Duplicate Your Top Advisors

Once you have identified who your best clients are and established where you can dominate, how do you duplicate them? You probably did not realize that you have a natural fit with your current client list. You will be amazed at the large percentage of your business that is connected to something common. That could be a platform, a firm, a partnership, or a geographic area. About fifteen years ago, I worked with a wholesaler in the Midwest. He had been wholesaling for many years. He was an average wholesaler at best. He was a large, beer drinking, cigarette smoking guy that was fun to be around, but not the most professional. His clientele was much like him. He was getting a lot of heat from management to pick up his sales. They were making his life miserable. He took a step back and said to himself, "how do I increase my sales without working harder?" He was not exactly the most motivated person. He went through his book and realized that much of his business was coming from a handful of advisors that had something in common. They concentrated their practices around retirement rollovers and 401k plans. He figured that if he only prospected these types of advisors and turned them into producers then his business would go up and management would get off his back. He went to his current clients with his plan and asked for their help. They taught him everything they knew about this market and took him out on appointments with them. Before he knew it he was taking the knowledge that he was learning from one team and educating another team. It was not long before he was an invaluable partner to these teams. He continued to read and learn everything about the rollover, 401k and 403b laws. He then narrowed his prospecting focus to other advisors with similar business practices. The following year he was a member of the "Top Producer's Club." He was still drinking, smoking and large, but nobody in his territory would present a qualified retirement plan without him. He became the market. He dominated!

Find your natural strength and play to it. Talk to your clients. Ask them for help. They are doing business with you because they like you. You have helped them. They will be more than happy to help you. Advisors feel great if they think they are helping you. It is human nature. I have also seen wholesalers build a "board" or "advisory" for their business. The clients seem to take some ownership and work to help the wholesaler grow their business.

Learn everything you can about that business. Know more about it than your clients. More importantly, know more about it than any of your competition. If you accomplish this you will become an invaluable resource. There will be no advisor worth their weight in gold who will not need your service and products. Use knowledge to dominate.

Divide Your Clients/ Prospects for Routing

You can have fantastic clients and boundless prospects, but if you do not segment your clientele into a well-organized routing system you will be doomed. Average wholesalers allow their clients to control their calendar, but successful wholesalers control their own schedule. Always remember that wholesaling, in its simplest form, is a numbers game. The more people you get in front of, the better your chances at success. The less people you see the greater chance of finding a new career. I continue to observe talented wholesalers that are still struggling to become a top producer or are wholesaling themselves out of the business. These wholesalers have all the education, skills, personality and the drive to be magnificent wholesalers, but they fail because they do not get in front of enough clients/prospects. The only reason why they do not see the volume they need to succeed is because they run an unorganized calendar.

Back in the late nineties I had a very good friend that wholesaled at the same firm as I did. His knowledge of the firm's products, managers and value added material was second to none. He had a very charismatic personality and had great relationships with his clients.

I remember attending sales conferences with our top advisors and listened to this wholesaler's clients singing his praise. He had achieved the greatest advantage you can have with a client. They were more than great clients, but they were close personal friends.

I was very jealous of the intimacy of his relationships. His wholesaling philosophy was to "never eat alone." He would have two to three meals a day with clients. He had all the necessary skills, drive and strategy to be a top wholesaler, but he was stuck in mediocrity.

It did not occur to me or him why he was not producing more until a phone conversation I had with him one morning. I will never forget it. I was in downtown Chicago. I was just leaving a breakfast meeting and was on my way to my next appointment one block away. My phone rang. It was my buddy in Ohio. He was also leaving a breakfast meeting. He said he had some "time to kill" between meetings. He told me that he was leaving Cleveland and on his way to Dayton for a lunch with an advisor. My response was "Dude, that is why you are stuck in the mud." I continued to tell him that while he was driving to Dayton, I had scheduled three meetings before my lunch meeting. As we talked it became obvious that this was a typical day. He was not going to eat alone. He would travel great distances between his appointments on a regular basis.

We talked about getting control of his calendar and building a routing system to make him more efficient and allow him to see more people. He agreed that was what he needed to do. Unfortunately, he was never able to secure control of his calendar and is still a midlevel wholesaler today. This guy has literally left millions of dollars on the table that could be in his pocket had he only developed a routing system and gained control of his calendar.

The idea of a routing system is uncomplicated. Divide your clients into geographic territories. If you are in a city, your geographic territory may be a couple of square blocks. In a rural area it may be neighboring towns. The whole idea is to limit your travel time to a minimum. Remember, "It's a numbers game." If you can limit you travel time and squeeze in an extra meeting, that's money. The more people you see the more you make.

How many "routes" is an individual preference? It is often dictated by your manager and your firm. Your manager, if worth his/her weight, should be able to examine your territory and determine the proper number of "routes." I personally liked eight weekly routes with one swing week. This meant my calendar would be set for a year in advance. I knew exactly when I was going to be back in an office, but more importantly my clients knew when I was going to be back. Advisors would call to find out when I was going to be back in their office. They knew I would be there a minimum of every other month. My calendar was set. I was maximizing my time and controlling my life. The swing week was designed for special circumstances, such as a seminar with a top producer, a 401k call with an advisor, a meeting with an important advisor that could not wait until my next visit, or perhaps your firm was having a push on a product or value added campaign. There will be times when you need to say no. It is always hard not to be responsive to all requests of your time. If you do not learn to say no then you will end up like my buddy in Ohio. Do not get stuck in the mud, control your schedule and your life. You will have more time and money. That is a good thing!

Anchor Your Day

Once you have done some extensive research of your clients and prospects you are prepared for a coverage strategy. Remember, you have identified a market that you wanted to dominate. When you schedule in a routing area you need to schedule an anchor meeting well in advance. This can be an office meeting, a team or advisor that you are targeting, a seminar, a dinner or a lunch with a top producer of yours. These meetings can be programmed months in advance.

Go back to my tactic of doing lunch meetings in large offices. Because I had a very exact routing system I knew when I was scheduled to be back in their office for the year. I would schedule my lunches for the entire year. This way I was not scrambling around for a lunch meeting or appointment just a few days before I was scheduled to be in the area. This is one of the principal blunders that wholesalers make.

For twenty-five years I have watched wholesalers take an office day on Friday to schedule for the following week. The chances of getting the quality meetings that you want, in that short notice, are "slim to none." It is a habit that most wholesalers fall into.

Scheduling meetings well in advance assures you of acquiring the meetings that you really covet. The easiest way to schedule would be to schedule meetings, in the office you are in, for the next time you're in that office. If I was in an office doing my scheduled meeting, I would not depart until I secured a meeting with a top team for the next time through that office.

Make that meeting special. Make it a meal, a game, a play or something out of the office. This way it is on their schedule. I once trained a wholesaler in New York City. She was a focused individual that had a strategy of out working all wholesalers. She also adopted the philosophy of seeing 150 advisors a week. Unlike me, she was not going to do it through lunch meetings. She did two things. First she worked a seven day work week. She would find advisors and their spouses that would meet her for golf, dinner or a play on the weekends. She would have parties where she would invite advisors. She took the idea of an anchor meeting to an extreme. She would have two or three anchor meetings every day. Looking at her "day planner" was like admiring a work of art. She color coded her meeting. Meals would be one color, retirement meeting would be another color and a large prospect would be another color. She would make sure to have all three colors scheduled every day. She would backfill meetings after that. She also would confirm every meeting two days in advance. To me, she was neurotic. To all the advisors she was very organized and professional. Nobody worked harder than her and her clients knew and respected her. I thought that she would eventually burn out. I was wrong. She not only is still a top producer twenty years later, but also found time to get her master's at night. She is an extraordinary wholesaler. Also, while most wholesaler's are having an office day so they can schedule, she was out seeing their clients. She has mastered the idea of anchor meetings and scheduling while in an office.

Choose the market that you want to dominate. Set up your routing system. Then anchor away.

Prospect, Prospect, Prospect

Prospecting is the lifeblood of successful wholesaling. Most people find it to be the worst part of wholesaling. Call me crazy. It is my favorite part of wholesaling. I get so excited for a prospecting call. I view it as tracking and hunting an animal. It is the hunt I love.

I believed that "an elephant a day would keep my manager away." I took steps to trap those elephants. I determined who the top advisors were in my territory. I learned as much as I could about them and their practice. I found a way to get an appointment with them (even if I had to use the "rubber chicken" strategy). I got everything in order. I was ready to trap my prey.

I always made sure that 50% of all my calls were prospecting. As I stated in earlier chapters, it is a numbers game. The more prospects you call on, the greater the chance for increased production. Of those 50% prospecting calls, one needed to be with an elephant.

An elephant is an advisor that can be a multi-million dollar producer. These advisors are easy to find, but usually difficult to penetrate. They are the advisors that usually occupy the corner office or they occupy a large suite. The nice part of our business is that top producers don't hide. The larger the office, the greater the production.

One of the biggest mistakes wholesalers make is that they cease their prospecting. In the early years we perform a lot of prospecting because we don't have clients yet. Once we get clients and are production is good wholesalers tend to spend most of their time servicing existing clients and not prospecting. Eventually some wholesaler's production blows right by that wholesaler. They wonder what happened. The answer is simple. The other wholesaler kept prospecting.

Think about the best advisors in your territory. I would be willing to bet that they still prospect. Think about the mid level producers. They are stuck in the mud trying to figure out why they fail to get to the next level. I would be willing to bet that they talk about how they need to start performing more prospecting but never do.

The same is true for wholesaling. The best wholesalers continually prospect. The mid level wholesaler knows that they need to do more prospecting, but do not do anything about it.

Prospecting has to be a constant. Do the math. How many prospect calls do you need to do in a day to be the top wholesaler? Who am I going to prospect? What do I know about the prospect and their practice?

Track them. Hunt them. Trap them. Be a master of prospecting and you will be successful forever.

Pits and Cherries

I know what you are thinking. How do I spend 50% of my time prospecting and have time to service and help my existing customers?

First of all, the 50% number was what I lived by. Your number could be 5%, 10% or 50%. You are probably saying; I still don't have enough time in the day as it is and now you are saying that I need to prospect more.

The answer is simple. You need to free up some time in the day.

The best way to free up some time is to dump some clients. That is a problematic thing to do. You have worked so hard to acquire them and now I am suggesting dumping them. It is what I call "Pits and Cherries."

The "Pits" are the clients that have not and will not reach a certain threshold of production. They can also be advisors that are above your threshold but suck too much time out of your day.

This is one of the first sales strategies that I learned and is still one of the most successful. You need to do some math. If you want to be a $400 million producer you need to figure out what your production threshold will be. For example, I would figure out how many clients that I would service. Then I would tier them into Tier 1, Tier 2 and Tier 3. I would set an annual production level of $5 million for my top 25 advisors. My Tier 2 would have production level of $2.5 million for my next 25 advisors. Tier 3 would be $1 million for the next 50 advisors.

The math works like this. I would figure the Tier 1 advisors would average $7.5 million in sales for an annual production of $187.5 million. Tier 2 advisors would average $3.5 million for $87.5 million in annual production and the Tier 3 advisors would average $1.5 million for an annual production of $75 million. Add all three tiers together and it equals $350 million in annual production. The remaining $50 million of sales would come from your prospects and "below threshold" advisors.

Each tier would get a different level of service. Tier 1 would get the Platinum service. Tier 2 would receive Gold service and Tier 3 would receive Silver service. If they were a "below threshold" advisor they would receive a majority of their coverage from my internal.

The top three tiers would get 50% of my meetings each day. They would receive 80% of my marketing budget beyond my office meeting costs.

In order for this strategy to be successful, you need to throw out the "Pits." The "Pits" are the advisors that do not reach your threshold. If they are up and coming advisors with the ability to get to your Tier levels, but have not reached them yet, they are still prospects. If an advisor is above your threshold, but do not warrant the time they demand of you and your internal then they become "Pits."

The whole idea with "Pits and Cherries" is to increase the levels of your Tiers. If you raise the level of your Tier 1 advisors from $5 million to $7.5 million, Tier 2 from $2.5 million to $3 million and Tier 3 from $1.5 million to $1.75 million you would boost your annual sales to approximately $525 million.

By spending your time on your uppermost advisors and prospects you will become more efficient with your time and resources. This will allow you to elevate the level of your prospecting and servicing and you will quickly and steadily raise the levels of your tiers and will become more and more successful.

Remember to throw out the "Pits" and keep the "Cherries."

Ritz Service

When developing your multiple levels of service, that will give you your "tiered" advisors, think about businesses that perform excellent service. So often we look for answers within our industry. I found that the best service companies existed outside our industry.

The company that I tried to emulate was The Ritz-Carlton Hotel. Many years ago I was covering St. Louis. The firm I was with was using "The Ritz" as their preferred hotel. (I tried to stay at a Marriott, but my firm told me that I was to stay at the Ritz-Carlton if there was one in the area.) The more that I lodged at the hotel the more it became obvious that their level of service was superior to all others. Not only were they there for all your desires, but it was the attention to detail that amazed me.

Being a big fan of the mini bar, I would enter my room after a long day of meetings and hit the mini bar. I would open the door and grasp a Coca Cola and some peanuts. As the night would go on I would drink all three of the Coca Colas in the mini bar. They would resupply the Coca Colas and peanut during the day and I would consume them again the next night. This occurred on consecutive trips to that hotel. That was nothing special. The Marriott's that I normally stayed at would do the same. It was the third time that I notice something different. When I checked in at the front desk the person who was checking me in not only welcomed me back, but said that they had over stocked my mini bar with Coca Colas and peanuts. They asked me if that was okay and said to let them know if I needed anything else.

When I entered my room I went directly to the mini bar. They had not only overstocked the mini bar with Coca Colas, but they had given me a larger refrigerator to fit a 12 pack of Coca Cola. As for those peanuts, not only had they supplied me with more of the same peanuts, they also had multiple variations of the traditional peanut. There was salted, unsalted, shelled and unshelled. I was in wholesaler heaven.

The next morning I woke up and vacated the room for a prosperous day of wholesaling. When I opened the door I noticed that not only did I have a Wall Street Journal hanging from my door knob, but there was also a Chicago Tribune. I found that interesting and impressive. Why was that interesting? It was interesting because I was in St. Louis. Why was I impressed? I was impressed because I was from Chicago. That attention to detail peaked my interest. I stopped by the front desk and asked them about the Chicago Tribune. The response from the concierge was; "Mr. Balch, we notice that you are from Chicago and though that you might want to see what was going on at home." I walked out of that hotel thinking how impressed I was with their service and thoughtful gestures.

That evening, after a couple of Coca Colas and a few peanuts I meandered down to the lobby to do a little snooping around. I started by observing the people milling about. I was astounded with how all the employees were all saying hello to the guests. When I say all employees I mean anyone that worked there. That included the maintenance people, housekeeping and the traditional lobby employees. Many times they would engage their guests by name. After sitting in the lobby for about five minutes one of the front desk people came over to me and said "good evening Mr. Balch." She wanted to know if she could get me anything. I was not looking for anything, but what the heck…I am at "The Ritz." I said that I would love a Coca Cola. She then asked "would you like a snack to go with the soda?" My response was "how about some peanuts?" With that she was off to the bar area. A few minutes later she was back with my Coke and peanuts.

I was so impressed with their service I needed to ask her how she knew my name. She started to tell me about their pre-shift meetings. She said that before every shift that all shift employees would preview the guest list. At the meeting they would review the guest's previous stays. In my case they knew that I had consumed only Cokes and peanuts in my previous stays, so they assumed that I would continue with that behavior. That is why they overstocked my mini bar with my favorites. They then check where I was from and got me my local paper if possible. If they could not get a guest's local paper they would pull the Web version of their paper off their computer. As far as remembering the guest's names, they are all told that is a skill that they need to learn. For what I could see they were very skilled. As we talked about the inner workings of the hotel she mentioned that their General Manager offers seminars on how the Ritz-Carlton services their guests and what goes into it.

After contemplating the extraordinary service that this hotel was giving its guests at no real additional cost, I started thinking how I could offer a "Ritz" like service to my clients. I determined that when I returned to Chicago I needed to contact the General Manager of the Chicago hotel to see if he/she also did seminars.

I contacted the General Manager and visited him to learn more about the seminar. I was very impressed with what he had to say. He explained about how they have the pre-shift meetings. That was in line with what I had heard about at the St. Louis Ritz. He also told me about how they empower all their employees. Each employee has a budget amount that they can use on a guest without asking for permission. This allows the employee to help a guest on the spot. If a guest has a need and they ask any employee for help, the employee can assist them on the spot without having to call anyone. The manager told me that this gives them a since of ownership. It is also very important for all their employees to recognize the guests and offer assistance. No matter which Ritz-Carlton property you visit, they will stop what they are doing to recognize the guest. What they do for the hotel did not matter; they are all ambassadors for the Ritz-Carlton. After hearing that I have taken notice to how all the employees at each property stop what they are doing and recognize you and offer their assistance.

I was so taken by their service model that I implemented many of the same concepts with my top producers. First I empowered my internal with reasonable requests. I gave him a dollar amount limit he could spend on a client without eliciting permission from me. The internal knew what I would spend on a client, what type of events I believed in, who I wanted to partner with vs. who just wanted money or golf balls. Now they were empowered to immediately assist with a client. This made the internal feel important and the client felt they were getting better service.

We also checked the requests of our top clients in the past. We found that most of them showed some kind of consistent behavior. Some asked for golf balls when the weather got nice, some did seminars at certain times of the year, some took their clients out to dinners during the holiday season, etc. We began to get in front of the impending request. Before they could ask us for golf balls or a seminar we would send them some balls or call them to offer our assistance with the seminars. They were very impressed that we knew so much about their business and what they liked. I would keep track of things that they had in their offices. If they had a candy jar sitting on their desk, I would send them candy refills. If they liked to read industry books, I would send them a copy of my favorite reads. If they played tennis, I would send them tennis balls. These were little gesture that got an enormous response. Proactive responses were much more impactful than the typical reactive approach.

I also used the General Manager to help my clients. I started to do small lunches at the Ritz-Carlton's in my territory. We would have the lunch in a small private room. During the lunch the General Manager would come in and do a quick presentation. The advisors loved it. Just like me they all got ideas on how they could improve their servicing. These lunches became so popular that advisors that did not live near a Ritz-Carlton would take a day off from their office to be a part of one of these meetings.

When servicing, sometimes we think that the industry standard is good enough. The reality is if you can differentiate your service from the completion the impact will amaze you.

Never Lose a Customer

Maybe I should rename this chapter "Never lose a customer that is within your control." There will always be events that happen you have no control over. There is nothing you can do if an advisor leaves their firm and moves to a firm that your firm does not have a selling agreement with.

If you have developed a well-diversified product relationship with your top clients you should never lose them. If one of your managers "blows up" you have relationship protection because you have diversified your products. Yes, it will strain the relationship. A top wholesaler will be able to fight through the turmoil and keep the relationship.

I will never forget a conversation I had with a very successful sales person I worked with at Fidelity Investments. This gentleman was the first sales person that was ever hired at Fidelity. Most of the companies within Fidelity had originated from him. He said when he first started he said that "if they had a smoke stack they were a potential client." If they were a bank he sold them mutual funds. If they were an insurance company he would sell them on the idea of wrapping their insurance around Fidelity's investment portfolios and sell annuity's to their clients. If they were a Fortune 500 firm he would sell them 401k's. He had something for everyone.

I had a tremendous amount of respect for everything he had accomplished. Even though he had management responsibilities, he was still a salesman. He was always selling. You knew he was trying to sell you something, but you enjoyed it.

I have endless stories about this gentleman and his successes. The one that stuck out with me was when I asked him how he built all his relationships. His answer was simple. He said "I have never lost a customer." He continued, "Through good and bad times I always found a way to hold onto my clients."

His point was that he spent so much time starting and developing the relationship. Why would he ever let that relationship get away? That is a lesson that we all should learn.

I have heard over and over from all wholesalers why they were losing clients. There was always a reason why they would let a client walk away. It was because of performance. It was because of marketing. It was because of their manager. It was because of (fill in the blank).

The only reason why we should let a client leave is if we can no longer, legally, sell to them. Saving clients from leaving is what makes a truly exceptional wholesaler. What made the gentleman truly exceptional was his ability to turn chicken poop into chicken salad. If Fidelity would be in jeopardy of losing an account they would call this man to save the relationship. Not only would he save the relationship, but he would find a way to sell that client something else. He would walk out of that situation with a stronger relationship than there was before.

The easy thing to do when adversity hits is to blame others and let the client walk. The hard thing is to face the issue. It can be difficult to defend your firm sometimes, but your clients will respect you more for facing the adversity head on.

Remember, if you have a good working relationship with that client they also are looking for a reason to keep the relationship. Get in their office and fight for what you spent so much time building. Have the mind set: "Never lose a customer."

Build a Blueprint

Over the years I have grown to hate the term "business plan." It is a preconceived notion that a business plan should be a long detailed document. I have worked at firms where we would spend the last two months of the year to write a business plan. We would write these long detailed plans. We would rewrite them. We would rewrite them again. We would finalize the plan and then hand them into our managers. The manager would send it to their manager. My manager's manager would send them to the firm's president. That would be the last time I would see or hear of the business plan until we started the exercise in futility the next year.

Now that I have stated my case against the "business plan" now let me tell you that you need one. It just needs to be a living document.

If you are going to drive from Seattle to New Orleans, you will need a road map. If you are preparing for a football game, you need a game plan. If you are preparing to build a house, you develop a blueprint.

To be successful at anything you need a plan. You need to ask yourself a question. "What is my goal and how am I going to get there." If you don't ask yourself that question and don't have a plan then you will eventually fail.

Without a plan you will run around chasing you tail. Without a road map you will get off track. Without a game plan you will not know what to do next. Without a blueprint you will not have a foundation for success.

Take the time to get away from your phone and people for a period of time and develop a blueprint. Set your goal and then think what it is going to take to get you there. Determine who your "pits" and "cherries" are going to be. That can be done by setting your "tier" advisors threshold. Do the math. What do you need from those advisors to get to your goal? This can be difficult because when you elevate your threshold you will find some of your "emotionally" favorite advisors falling below the line. While these advisors may be close friends, they cannot warrant quality time from you. If you do not make that decision, then it will hamper your chances to reach your goal. You need to replace those advisors with better producers.

Who are those advisors that are above the threshold that are sucking too much time out of your day? You need to decide if you need to cut them loose or if you can cover them with less time. Just the other day I was visiting some of my past advisors doing some research. I had an appointment with an advisor that I used to do some business with about five years ago. I liked this advisor but had to cut him loose because he was sucking too much time from my internal and me. This was an advisor that was just above my lowest threshold, but demanded a weekly analysis of multiply products on multiply platforms. My internal and I figured that we were spending about 1 ½ hours per week on this advisor. I decided to cut him loose to make room for other prospects.

We were discussing many issues about wholesaling. The conversation turned to the topic of servicing. I could see that he was feeling uncomfortable. I told him to lay it out there. I needed to have his responses. He said that I was an awful servicer. He went on and told me that because I would not do his weekly analysis he had to find another wholesaler that would. He went on to show me how he used this analysis in his practice. Since he became a "pit" he had increased his analysis demands on wholesalers. After he got everything off his chest I asked him who his top wholesalers were. The three people he named were all lower end wholesalers. He showed me the reports that they were doing for him. They were very detailed and very impressive. They also would have taken a lot of man hours to produce them. After we wrapped up the meeting I left his office and a big smile hit my face. All I could think was I am glad that I had cut him loose. He would have sucked my time dry. As for the three wholesalers that he is now doing business with, I suggest cutting him loose if you want to raise your production. Their time would be better spent on prospects with greater potential.

Build your list of prospects. Who are your prospects? Do these prospects have the chance to be top tier advisors in your practice?

Once you build your list of prospects then you need a game plan on how you are going to convert them into "cherries". Just like a football coach that watches a lot of film preparing for a game a wholesaler needs to do the same with the prospects. Do you have enough information on that prospect? Can you get the information you need to build a game plan to compete for that prospects business?

Once you determine that you have all the information to acquire these prospects now you need to figure out how much time you will need to seal the deal. In your blueprint you need to build a foundation for solid prospecting. You need to determine how much of your day is going to be committed to prospecting.

Make sure that you build room to learn and better your skills. What are you going to do to make yourself more valuable to your clients? Are you going to get an additional license? Are you going to take some classes? Are you going to work on your presentation skills? You need to keep improving to stay on top. Michael Jordan would add a new move or shot to his basketball game every off season. Just when everyone thought they knew how to defend him, he would develop a new weapon to defeat them. It is important to stay ahead of the competition.

What is your marketing plan going to be? What value added programs does your firm offer? What programs are they developing that you can use next year? What program have you developed? What program can you develop?

You need a marketing road map. If you don't, you will be all over the map. Develop a marketing plan that is focused in on your "tiered" advisors and prospects. Stay focused on that map. If you look at most successful wholesalers you will find that they have a focused marketing plan. They know who their clients and prospects are. They take a rifle shot approach to them.

What products does your firm offer? How diversified are you with your clients? How can I cross sell my product line? How can I sell the "out of favor" products?

It is both easier and important to sell the "flagship" products. These are products that you need to open doors and raise assets. If you have a hot product it is important to take advantage of the situation. The door will not be open forever. Make hay while you can. If you are selling predominately growth products then you need to put a game plan together to sell your value products. If you are selling mostly fixed income, you need a plan to deliver more equity. If we have learned anything about the markets, we have learned that the world can change overnight. In order to sustain longevity in this business you need to diversify your product mix. Plan on how much time you need to devote to each product. If you don't then you will find yourself selling primarily what is "hot." You might look at your product mix and feel that you can't sell certain products because other firms have better products in that space. Remember, advisors do business with people not products. You may not sell a ton of that product, but your time selling it will be worth its weight in gold if the markets turn away from you.

Now that you have thought about what needs to go into your "business plan," how do I write it as a living document? It is simple. Just build an outline.

Clients

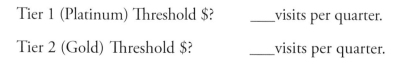

    Tier 1 (Platinum) Threshold $?   ___visits per quarter.

    Tier 2 (Gold) Threshold $?   ___visits per quarter.

Tier 3 (Silver) Threshold $?   ____visits per quarter.

How much budget money will you spend on these clients?

Prospects

Elephants...   How many meetings each week?

Prospects...   How many contacts each day?

How much budget money will you spend on these prospects?

Products

"Flagship 1" $_____

"Flagship 2" $_____

"Diversified Product 1" $_____

"Diversified Product 2" $_____

"Out of Favor Product 1" $_____

"Out of Favor Product 2" $_____

Marketing

What value added products?

Money Manager/Research travel in territory?

Seminars?

Lunch meetings?

Education

Classes?

Licenses?

Tutors?

It is important to build a "simple" blueprint. After you build a living outline of what you need to do to accomplish your goals, take that plan and have it laminated. Once laminated, put that plan in your bag and look at it every day. It will act as a road map to what you need to do every day. If you follow it every day you will stay on course.

The reason why you look at it every day is because it will keep you on task. It will remind you to sell the "out of favor products" when it is easy not to. It will remind you that you need to schedule an elephant. It will remind you to set up seminars. It will remind you to spend time with the "cherries" and not the "pits." It will remind you to take that presentation class.

Build a blueprint for success. If you don't you will get off track and be lost. We are pulled in a million differ directions. It is important to stay focused on what is important for your success. A working document will protect you from distractions.

Think Outside the Box

We often get stuck looking at our business with blinders on. We usually limit our ideas to things that we have seen and used in our business before. If something works for one wholesaler we all adopt the idea until we are all using the same idea. We often retread old ideas that worked in the past. You should always find ideas that are working for others and adopt them into our practice. It is always smart to use ideas that have proven to work in similar situations. If this is the only place where you get ideas then you run the risk of getting "bland".

I believe that we have been conditioned to be "bland." There is reason for this. Being "bland" is safe. Being "bland" is politically correct. Being "bland" protects you from getting embarrassed. Being "bland" is a recipe for bad marketing. Jon Spoelstra wrote in his book, *Marketing Outrageously*, "bland" doesn't make a buyer think. Bland doesn't touch the emotions of buyers. Bland doesn't motivate the buyer to buy." Spoelstra goes on to say "marketing bland does work, however. It works when competing against other bland marketing. Then, whoever has the biggest pile of bland usually wins." How true this is. Remember, we are a commodity. We often keep piling on to the large mound of marketing ideas. We feel if we have more ideas, even though they are also being used by others, the better off we will be.

I challenge you to be unique. Someday I will write a book on this subject. What separate's good wholesalers from great wholesalers is their ability to think "outside the box" to gather ideas and strategies. In a "me too" business if you do not find fresh ideas you may have success as a wholesaler, but you will not be a top producer. It is important to get creative. Find an idea that is going to get the attention of your clients. If you get their attention, then you will earn the opportunity to present yourself and your firm to them. I like to spend time in book stores reading articles in magazines like "Entrepreneur" and "Inc." There are always articles about successful people and businesses. They often write about how they broke into the business to capture market share from the more established businesses. It is also a good idea to comb the marketing section of the bookstore for ideas. Typically if a person has become successful in their business there is a book written about them. Some books have so many good ideas that it is worth purchasing.

Here is an example of how I found an idea that I incorporated into my marketing plan. In Spoelstra's book he wrote a chapter entitled "The Rubber Chicken Method."

> The chapter goes like this; Rick Benner was down for the count. After reviewing his season ticket renewal figures in the summer 1998, the president of the Sacramento Kings felt beat up – not physically, but emotionally. It looked like 4,000 of the King's season-tickets subscribers – 40 percent – would not renew.
>
> Kings fans felt a little beat up, too. They had endured fourteen straight losing seasons, the longest any pro team had ever gone without coming

out ahead. Until the summer of 1998, however, the fans had kept buying season tickets – better than 90 percent renewals every year, in fact.

To make things even worse, the team could do nothing to improve itself. The NBA had imposed an indefinite labor lockout. NBA teams couldn't sign a free agent, couldn't trade. If you finish the season with a lousy team, you were stuck with a lousy team during the all-important marketing period. You had to market your lousy team without the one priceless tool that was available to pro teams: perennial hope that the team would get better.

The Kings had already sent three mailings to season ticket holders who had not renewed. The fourth letter, according to the Kings' pattern, would be a "drop dead" letter. This was a letter in wordy legalese, sent to a hundred or so non-renewers to clear their seats for new buyers. It said, in effect, "You no longer have any rights to your season tickets. See ya."

As a marketing consultant to the Sacramento Kings, I was alarmed. This would be the last nail in the coffin for 4,000 season tickets. With 40 percent non-renewers staring us in the face, how could we stop this death spiral? I felt that the Kings fans were terrific fans, maybe the most loyal fans in the league. They had, after all, bought season tickets through fourteen straight losing seasons. But now 40 percent of them were saying, "Enough is enough!" Those fans needed special attention – something to reassure then that management would somehow deliver a competitive team.

I went to Rick and asked him not to send the drop-dead letter. I suggested another approach. I showed him a letter I had drafted. Unlike the other letters, which had been written by accountants and lawyers and sounded that way, this was letter was honest with the fan. It didn't hedge; it stated our problems – and solutions – in straight forward language.

Rick liked the letter. But, he said, there was a problem. "Our fans won't even open the letter. They never open any of our letters."

"That is because they were boring and vague," I said. "They were lousy reading. But I can get them to open this one. I'll guarantee it."

"How are you going to do that?" he asked. Then he remembered a story from my book *Ice to the Eskimos*. "Not the Rubber Chicken?"

I nodded. "The Rubber Chicken."

It was a rubber chicken, three feet long, which was stuffed in a tubular FedEx package. The chicken had a little paper jersey. On one side, the jersey read, "Don't fowl out!" on the other, "You're about to fowl out! However, you can avoid the bench and keep playing. Just read the attached."

The "attached" was our letter, inside an envelope tied to the chicken's leg.

It took just one day to find out what the response would be. A few of our grumpier fans thought we had insulted them – but many of them renewed their season tickets anyway. They had read the letter and liked what we had to say. Many more fans were amused; they called laughing to renew.

Some fans that had already renewed called and said, "How come they didn't get a rubber chicken?" We sent them their own personal rubber chicken.

A sports columnist at the local newspaper, the *Sacramento Bee*, got a rubber chicken:

I've seen a lot of things in my day, Mister. I have seen grown men and woman cry over games. I've seen courage and I've seen cowardice. I have seen feats of majesty and precociousness and minutiae and enduring value, all in the name of sports. In a reflective moment' I fancy that I've nearly seen it all.

Then again, no NBA team ever sent me a rubber chicken in the mail.

The Rubber Chicken accomplished its mission. I'm pretty sure everybody who got a rubber chicken read the letter. They'd have to. If you received a letter attached to a rubber chicken, you'd probably read it too.

Did it work? It definitely helped. It cost about $12 to send each chicken. We got 1,000 extra renewals, worth about $2.5 million in revenue.

And that – heh, heh – ain't chicken feed.

That was an entertaining story, but you might be thinking, what does that have to do with wholesaling? After sitting in a Barnes and Noble store reading that chapter I wondered if I could adapt the "Rubber Chicken" in my practice. After thinking about it, I had an idea. I said to myself, "who would benefit from this strategy?"

This would be an idea for those advisors that won't give me any time on the phone or in the office. I started by sending a rubber chicken to the top producers in an office where I was going to do a lunch meeting. These were producers that never attended lunch meetings and would not meet with me in the office. I sent them a chicken with two signs attached to them. One side read, "Don't fowl out!" The other side said, "Avoid missing out of an idea that will increase your production." I would send these chickens, for delivery, the day before the meeting. The responses were outstanding. The first time I sent a chicken is still my favorite. The advisor who never met with wholesalers and was very surly barged into my lunch meeting holding the rubber chicken by the neck and said "what's up with this bird?" I told him that he could either join the lunch meeting or I could meet with him immediately after the meeting. He said "fine, stop by when you are done."

I stopped by after the lunch meeting and presented him with a marketing strategy that had been produced by our marketing department. We spent about one hour together that day and he eventually became one of my better producers.

The response was outstanding. I would get calls from advisors wanting to know why I was sending them a rubber chicken. I got calls from advisor's assistants telling me that their advisor would be busy that day but wanted to schedule time with the advisor on a different day. Many just came to the lunch meeting. But all them opened the package and read the note.

The "Rubber Chicken" might seem childish or outrageous but I was interacting with top producer that I could never get to before. I had moved beyond "bland." I had separated myself from the pack. The idea may have been outrageous, but it was highly successful.

Think outside the box. If you don't, you will be bland. Remember what Spoelstra says about being bland. "Bland is safe. Bland is politically correct. Bland is not getting laughed at. Bland is bad marketing."

Position Yourself

What do your clients and prospects think of you? How are you positioned in the minds of your clients and prospects? Are you just another wholesaler? Are your products just like all other products in the minds of your clients and prospects? How is your firm positioned in the mind of the advisor? The key to this chapter is to learn how to position yourself, your firm and your products in the mind of the advisor.

We need to understand the world of communication in our business. While we live in a world of over communication, very little communication actually takes place. We just throw a lot of noise at the advisor but fail to communicate a very simple strategy to position ourselves in the advisors mind. The battle is not for selling all our wonderful products to the clients, but the battle is for a place in their minds. You will never sell much until you get yourself positioned properly in their minds.

There is a timeless book called *Positioning: The Battle for Your Mind* written by Al Reis and Jack Trout. Every wholesaler should own this book. It does a wonderful job of explaining the many different ways to position yourself, your products and your firm in the minds of the advisor.

In their book, Reis and Trout write:

"In our over communicated society, the paradox is that nothing is more important than communication. With communication going for you, anything is possible. Without it, nothing is possible. No matter how talented and ambitious you may be.

What's called luck is usually an outgrowth of successful communication. Saying the right things to the right person at the right time. Finding what the NASA people in Houston call a window in space.

Positioning is an organized system for finding a window in the mind. It is based on the concept that communication can take place at the right time and under the right circumstances."

I felt so strong about the idea of positioning and "winning the battle for the advisor's mind" that every day I would remind myself that it was all about positioning. Just like a golfer that thinks about a couple of things before they start their swing. Just like a skier would visualize their run before starting. I used positioning to trigger my day. How could I position myself in the mind of my advisors? That then triggered my mind for the day of appointments.

I would like to share some of my firm, product and personal positioning ideas I used over the years with great success.

In Reis and Trout's book they talk about "repositioning the competition." They write:

With a plethora of products in every category, how does a company use advertising to blast its way into the mind? The basic underlying marketing strategy has got to be "reposition the competition."

In other words, to move a new idea or product into the mind, you must first move an old one out.

"The world is round," said Christopher Columbus. "No, it's not," said the public, "it's flat."

To convince the public otherwise, fifteenth century scientists first had to prove that the world wasn't flat. One of their more convincing arguments was the fact that sailors at sea were first able to observe the tops of the masts of an approaching ship, then the sails, then the hull. If the world were flat, they would see the whole ship at once.

All the mathematical arguments in the world weren't as effective as a simple observation the public could verify themselves.

Once an old idea is overturned, selling the new idea is often ludicrously simple. As a matter of fact, people will often actively search for new ideas to fill the void.

Never be afraid to conflict either. The crux of a repositioning program is undercutting an existing concept, product, or person.

Conflict, even personal conflict, can build a reputation overnight. Where would Sam Ervin have been without Richard Nixon?

For that matter, where would Richard Nixon have been without Alger Hiss?

And Ralph Nader got famous not by saying anything about Ralph Nader but by going out and attacking the world's largest corporation single-handedly.

People like to watch the bubble burst.

Many years ago, Tylenol was trying to gain market share in the aspirin space. The market was dominated by power houses such as Anacin, Bayer, Bufferine and Excedrin. How could they reposition all those heavy weights? The solution was quite simple; they needed to reposition the entire aspirin marketplace.

According to Reis and Trout:

> Tylenol went out and burst the aspirin bubble.
>
> "For the millions who should not take aspirin," said Tylenol's ads. If your stomach is easily upset… or you have an ulcer… or you suffer from asthma, allergies, or iron-deficiency anemia, it would make good sense to check with your doctor before you take aspirin."
>
> "Aspirin can irritate the stomach lining," continued the Tylenol ad, "trigger asthmatic or allergic reactions, cause small amounts of hidden gastrointestinal bleeding."
>
> "Fortunately, there is Tylenol…"
>
> Sixty words of copy before any mention of the advertiser's product.
>
> Sales of Tylenol acetaminophen took off. Today Tylenol is the No. 1 brand of analgesic. Ahead of Anacin. Ahead of Bayer. Ahead of Bufferin. Ahead of Excedrin. A simple but effective repositioning strategy did the job.

Against an institution like aspirin. Amazing.

What I took from that strategy was very useful in my ability to gather new clients at Fidelity Advisors, one on my past employers. I had just taken over a territory that ranked about 15th among all wholesalers in the Broker/Dealer channel. That was middle of the road. When I first got in the field I realized there was a strong dislike for Fidelity. The underlying distain was because the advisor viewed Fidelity as a competitor. Not only were they considered a competitor, but they believed that they were taking their clients.

I needed to reposition our firm in their minds. I needed to be able to show them that we, like our competitors in the advisor distribution business, had the ability to grow their business. I needed to find a way for them to do our products. After thinking about how Tylenol was able to reposition theirselves in a marketplace, and then dominate once they were accepted in the aspirin world.

It was true that many of the advisors clients and prospects were doing mutual fund business at Fidelity. Instead of sticking my head in the sand I used their fears as an opportunity to grow their business.

I started every meeting with an attention grapping line. I would say "Your customers are going to do business with Fidelity whether you like it or not." I continued, "Are they going to do it through you or someone else?"

I had repositioned how they felt about Fidelity. They went from avoiding Fidelity like the plague to embracing the idea that I could help them take assets from Fidelity Investments.

Once they realized that their clients were thrilled that they could get Fidelity funds from their advisor they started to prospect with Fidelity. That repositioning strategy took me from the middle of the pact to the top three and earned me an annual invitation to the firms "Leadership Club."

Another example of how I used *Positioning* by Ries and Trout is how I started selling a product that had $0 in sales when I took over a territory for Nations Funds, the Bank of America Asset Manager. They had acquired a great money manager from Janus Capital a year earlier. His track record was sparkling but people thought that he was too aggressive for their clients. He ran a concentrated portfolio style that was very different from the larger more popular funds that held over 100 names in their portfolios.

The competitor's funds were very successful. Even though we had a superior track record the advisor was happy with what they were holding. I needed a way to get them to consider using my manager, Tom Marsico.

I went back to the book by Reis and Trout and found an interesting positioning strategy. They talked about the Cola industry and how 7-Up found success in the soda world.

> "Another classic positioning strategy is to worm your way onto a ladder owned by someone else. As 7-Up did. The brilliance of this idea can only be appreciated when you comprehend the enormous share of mind enjoyed by Coke and Pepsi. Almost two out of every three soft drinks consumed in the United States are cola drinks.

By linking the product to what was already in the mind of the prospect, the "uncola" position established 7-Up as an alternative to a cola drink. (The three rungs on the cola ladder might be visualized as: One, Coke. Two, Pepsi, and three, 7-Up.)"

What 7-Up had done was to reposition itself into another space. In the mind of the soda drinker they had just given them an alternative to the colas that they have been drinking. They had opened up and entirely new market place.

In the minds of the drinkers, there were the cola brands such as Coke, Pepsi, Rite and all the other brown colas. 7-Up started a marketing strategy of the "uncola." They wanted the consumer to know that there was more to the Soda market than Coke and Pepsi.

It worked. Americans started to try the alternative uncola. Their sales went through the roof. Since the soda drinkers have found the uncola market soft drinks have exploded. Following 7-Up into the new space were drinks like Snapple and Gatorade. Now there is Red Bull and other power drinks. Without the "uncola" campaign, who knows where the soft drink business would be today? Maybe it would still be only Coke and Pepsi.

I took this strategy and applied it to my product versus the competition. I decided that I needed to reposition the fund into its own space. I needed the advisor to open their mind to another idea.

I went out and explained to the clients that our "growth fund" was very different from the ones that they were using. I explained that the other growth funds were the colas of the mutual fund business.

I then told them that there was an alternative market for growth investors. I called our product the "unfund." I wanted to open their minds to the world of concentrated portfolios.

It worked. I took a new product with $0 sales in my territory to over $250 million in sales the first year. I used that strategy and continue to grow my sales every year. During that period I was the top producer, net and gross, for seven years.

There are so many ways to position your firm, your products and yourself. You need a positioning strategy. Look outside the box to other industries and businesses. I simple strategy can catapult your sales to new heights. What is your positioning strategy?

Make Your Clients Money.

The best wholesalers make money for their clients. Ask yourself the question. Am I making money for my clients? I have found that the answer is usually NO! Most wholesalers are concerned most with making money for themselves and their firm. While it is fundamentally correct to want to make money for themselves and their firm, is that mind set putting the cart before the horse?

The wholesalers that make the most money for themselves and their firms over a long period of time have the mindset of making money for their clients. They put the horse in front of the cart.

When spending time with your advisors try to find out how you can increase their production. How do they prospect? How do they find clients? What are they doing to increase assets with their current clientele? What are they doing to maximize their time and their skills?

Find solutions for these questions and you will be well on your way to a long and prosperous relationship with that advisor.

The best way to make money for your clients is to find them clients. As a wholesaler you see and know most of the advisors to your territory. You probably asked yourself the question, who would I give my money to? Who would I recommend to my parents?

We have friends and family members that could use our help. If you had a friend that was sick and you knew the top doctor in the field that could help them, would you recommend that doctor? Of course you would. Why wouldn't you recommend the best advisors to your friends? We have invaluable knowledge and should share that with friends and family.

About ten years ago I had a friend that wholesaled in Minnesota. He was in town one weekend. I invited him and a friend out for a game of golf. He also brought his college roommate, who he was visiting. Somehow the conversation on the course turned to some of the suspect practices that were happening in our industry. The wholesaler asked his college roommate who his advisor was. He then asked me if I knew him. I didn't. He then asked his friend what his advisor does for him. The answer was "not much." He told his friend that that was not a good answer. He explained what the best advisors do for their clients. He then went on to tell him that he should talk to other advisors. With that he looked at me and said "who would recommend in the area?"

I immediately thought about two great advisors that had a lot in common with the wholesaler's college roommate. I told him about the two advisors that I was thinking about. I then asked him if he would like me to introduce him to them. He appreciated that I would do that for him.

My friend said to me, "we have been friends for years and you never did that for me." He continued, "You just met this guy and gave him the holy grail." With that the wholesaler asked me if I recommend advisors to my friends and family.

He told me that I was missing a great opportunity. I had the chance to help my friends and family and would benefit greatly by bringing clients to my advisors.

The next Monday I introduced the two gentlemen to two different advisors. They both hit it off. They both transferred over their accounts over the next few weeks and they have had a great relationships with each advisor ever since.

Ever since that round of golf, I have continued to recommend friends and family to advisors. These advisors are so thankful that I brought them clients. My relationship and production with these advisors have skyrocketed since I brought them business.

That is a small example of how we can make our clients money. There are many ways to make your clients money.

I had a friend whole specialized in retirement plans. He worked with his marketing and compliance group to build a seminar that he could deliver to small business owners. He then found an attorney that specialized with small business owners. He and the attorney developed a very informative seminar.

The wholesaler then took the seminar to his best clients. He suggested small seminars for the advisor's small business owners. The advisor's loved the idea. The wholesaler was so confident that this seminar would work that, in the beginning, he would pick up the entire cost of the seminar.

He was right. The advisor delivered the clients. He and the

attorney delivered the seminar. The clients delivered their retirement plans and more.

He made his clients more money with their existing book.

There are many ways to make your clients money. Just be aware of where you can help deliver clients, support and ideas. If you make your clients money then everything else will fall into place. If you put the horse before the cart then you and your firm will make a ton of money.

Be Proud to be a Wholesaler

I love being a wholesaler. It is the second greatest job I could have. The first would to be a professional athlete. Unfortunately, I did not have the tools to be a professional athlete, but I do have the right tools to be a great Wholesaler.

Over the years I have heard people asking wholesalers what they do for a living? Why do they wholesale? What do they want to be after wholesaling? Most of the time, the wholesalers response is vague and uninspiring. Folks, we have a great job. When I first got in the business I had a veteran wholesaler explain it to me this way. He said to think about all the people that you graduated college with. How many of those people are making the living that you are. If they are, they are probable successful doctors or lawyers. If they are lawyers or doctor, how do their hours compare to yours. Another veteran said that wholesaling was like having your own business without the overhead. He said that you work out of your own house. Set your own schedule and can make as much as you want. Both of those wholesalers had good points. Think about it. Where else can you wake up in the morning, go visit your friends and make the money we make? If you do not love wholesaling, then move over and let the next person in.

When I was growing up, or when I was in school, did I ever say that I want to "grow up and be a wholesaler?" No, in kindergarten I wanted to be a monkey. Eventually I grew out of that stage and started dreaming of being a fireman, astronaut, veterinary or a pro hockey player. Things happen, things change. Before I knew it I was a wholesaler. I am not sure how the path led me to this profession. Had I known what I know today I would have grown up saying that I wanted to be a wholesaler.

Like many who had my success selling, I eventually became a manager. I did that for a few years. My ego liked the fact that my business card said "SALES MANAGER." My brain said why do I want to lose control of my schedule, assume other people's problems, travel so much, make less money and not control my own destiny. The answer was easy. The last management decision I made was to hire myself as a wholesaler. I love wholesaling.

Many wholesalers believe that we just sell products. If that is the case, then you will lead a much uninspired career. Do you think the most satisfied heart surgeons just transplant hearts, or do they save lives? Do satisfied teachers just teach their subject, or do they inspire their students. The same holds true for wholesalers. Do we just sell products, or do we make the lives and practices of our clients better. The most satisfying time in my year is when advisors are putting together their business plans for the following year and they call me to get my advice.

There are still advisors, not in my territory, who ask for my help in building their business plan. To me that is satisfying. While the money is great, nothing is more satisfying than knowing that I am having an impact in someone's practice and life. I also love that moment when a client goes from customer to friend. When do know when that happens? It happens when your greetings go from handshakes to hugs. I will never forget the time one of my regional sales managers was traveling with me. We went to visit one of my best clients. This was a client that I have worked with for years. When we walked in his office my client shook my boss's hand and gave me a big bear hug. After the meeting my boss told me that he thought that the client was unprofessional to greet me that way and vice versa. All I could think was how unfortunately it was that he has gone through his entire wholesaling career without inspiring his clients.

Be proud to be a wholesaler!

Set the Bar High

I have never met a successful wholesaler that does not set their bar high. It is human nature to let up once you have achieved a goal. How many times have you heard an advisor say that they have hit their monthly, quarterly or annual goal and were setting up business for the next month, quarter or year?

Sprinters running the 100-meter dash don't run past the finish line and run another 100-meters. Goals are exactly that, Goals. Once you achieve the goal then you let up and "jog it in."

Your manager and firm will typically set goals for you and your territory. I suggest that you set your own goal. Here is a small suggestion. Set your goal higher than your firm set for you. Give yourself a prize for achieving that goal. Think about something that you really want to do, but cannot justify doing it. Perhaps you have always wanted to travel to an exotic location, but never could find the time. Perhaps you have always wanted season tickets to some sports team or the opera, but could never justify the expense.

If you set the bar high and achieve the goal then you will find the time and money to enjoy the prize. The only way this works is not to lie to yourself. The second you achieve your goal reserve

the trip or the tickets. Don't wait. If you do then you will rationalize why you shouldn't do it. Eventually the goal won't mean
anything to you. Put the carrot out there and eat it.

I always set a high goal for myself. Once I achieved my firm's
goal I would pat myself on my pack. That was not a very special
prize. I was rewarded by achieving the firm goals with trips, tro-
phies and stock. That was nice, but I wanted more for myself. I
worked hard to achieve my goals, but there was no impact prize.

One of my best friends would take some of the most interesting trips every year. He was doing extreme trips before they became popular. Every year he would come back from his trips with
pictures. He would make me sit through his slide show. He always had the "time of his life." It looked like a blast, but it seemed
extreme. I couldn't rationalize how I could take such a trip.

One year I noticed that he was not taking a trip. I asked him
why he was not taking a trip that year. He told me that he did not
meet his personal goal. He said that he had his best year ever, but
did not achieve his goal. He said that if he went on an exotic trip
that year then his goal would mean nothing. The next year he set
his goal and achieved it. He went on the most exotic trip ever.

Before he left on that trip I asked if he had set a more reasonable goal so that he would be able to go on the trip. He told me
that it was exactly the opposite. He had set the most aggressive
goal yet. He felt that if achieved it then he would reward himself
with the most exotic trip ever. He said there was nothing that was
going to keep him from his dream trip.

Think of a prize that will drive you. Set the bar high. Drive yourself to run through the corporate goal. Keep sprinting until you achieve your goals. Enjoy the rewards. Select the next carrot. Set the bar even higher and start sprinting!

You need to find something that is going to drive you to set the bar higher and higher. If you achieve your firm's goals and your goals, then it has indeed been a rewarding year.

Attitude Sells

This may be the most impactful part of this book. Remember the age old adages, "first impressions are the most lasting" – William Cosgrove. Another one is "You never get a second chance to make a first impression" – W. Triesthot. Not only is your first impression very important, but each time you see a client the "first impression" impact happens again. It is so important to be positive and confident the moment you walk in the door until you leave the building. My kid's orthodontist, while trying to sell me on why my child needs braces, told me that "a firm hand shake and a nice smile make a long lasting impression." How true that is. Your attitude is your calling card to who you are. You must realize that your attitude is very visual. Almost immediately, your clients will determine what your attitude is towards them. This will be demonstrated though emotions, opinions, actions and how you carry yourself. Your clients will respond to your attitude. If you have a positive attitude, your clients will have a positive attitude. If you are negative or disinterested, your clients will be negative or disinterested. Your clients will mirror their attitude with yours.

When you meet a current client or a prospect make sure you make eye contact, offer a nice smile and give them a firm hand shake. I may sound like your parents, but it may be the most important thing you do in that meeting. I just met with a long time client the other day. The market was getting "killed." The credit system was failing and it was snowing. This was not a good day. I walked into the gentleman's office. I gave him a smile and a firm hand shake and asked "how are the kids doing?" He said "you are breath of fresh air." He went on to tell me that I was the first wholesaler to walk into his office that week that did not tell him how difficult their day has been. You have to remember that the client was making calls and answering questions, all day, about the negative performance of his customer's portfolios. In a very dark day you need to be a ray of sunlight. We spent the meeting talking about family and things that were happening outside the office. I also gave him the some third party ideas about what was happening with the market. The meeting stayed positive. When I left his office, he had a little hop in his step and a smile on his face.

It is so important to be positive. When things are going well in the marketplace this is not difficult, but when things are tough it is easy to fall into the "negative trap." In tough markets it is normal for an advisor to be negative. It is a "trap" that the wholesaler must stay above. Be sensitive of an advisor's feelings, but do not add to the advisor's issues. Stay positive and find a subject matter that has a more positive tone.

Many advisors like to talk negative of other advisors, their firm and/or their management. Be very careful. Do not go down this path with the advisor. If you agree with their opinion, there is always the chance that your comments will get back to the wrong party. Also, if you are willing to make negative comments about others the advisor may wonder if you are saying negative things about them when you are visiting others. Be the person that is above all the negativity.

If your clients perceive that you are enthusiastic about what you are doing they will believe that you have their best interest at heart and will respond positively. In today's relationships, positive builds and attracts, while negative destroys and repels. If you stay positive and caring you will go a long way at removing skepticism from their minds. If you are in the "negative trap" the more re-pelled the people will become and the less likely they are to have confidence in you.

Be a Leader
Be in Charge

A top wholesaler is a leader. There are many reasons for this. Advisors are not looking for people to walk in and ask what "they can do for the advisor." The advisor hears that too often. They will usually give some stock answer like support, manager changes, money, etc. The advisor is looking for someone that is going to walk into their office and deliver ideas, knowledge, products and value. Remember, top advisors are also leaders of people. They are proactively taking ideas to their clients. Wholesalers need to do the same. Leaders hang with leaders. Generals hang with Generals, not with the enlisted.

Take charge of all your meetings. If you get time with an advisor or get an office meeting… own that moment. Do not waste that valuable time being like everyone else that preceded you. Be different, be bold, and be in charge. The advisor will respect you for that.

Recently, I have spent time visiting hundreds of advisors gathering information for this book. The one thing that rings true with most the advisors is that they want someone that can walk in their office and make their practice better. The advisor is not looking to give the wholesaler direction. It does not have to be an earth shattering revelation. It can be simple. Just the other day an advisor was telling me about a wholesaler who caught his attention in his first meeting with this wholesaler. The advisor, like many top producing advisors, does not usually see new wholesalers (That will be another chapter.). This wholesaler earned the meeting on the request of another advisor in the office. The advisor was expecting another typical "data dump." The wholesaler had done his homework before the meeting and had engaged the advisor in a very knowledgeable conversation about the advisors investment decisions. In the middle of the conversation, the wholesaler asked the advisor if he could show him something that would "back up his thoughts" on the advisor's computer. The advisor agreed. With that the wholesaler walks over to his "Work Station" and proceeded to navigate to pages that the advisor had never seen before. They spent the next 45 minutes navigating through the system gaining information that will help the advisor with his clients. The wholesaler not only customized the pages, but also included his products when applicable. The advisor told me that his meeting with that wholesaler was the "best hour he ever spent with a wholesaler." Since the meeting, he has included one of the wholesaler's products in each proposal he made since their meeting. He was so impressed with the wholesaler that he immediately walked down the hall to the referring advisor and bought him lunch. The wholesaler walked into that advisors office and took charge. He led the advisor somewhere he had never been before. What the wholesaler did was not "brain surgery," but it showed leadership. He added value and earned the business.

Another place where the wholesaler needs to show leadership is in an office meeting. You have their presence for a period time.

The question is do you have their attention? Most do not. The advisors expectations are very low. They advisor is expecting another dull data dump from someone just going through the motions. Be that wholesaler that walks into that meeting and takes charge. Take that meeting somewhere that others have not gone. Have a plan and deliver a brief, concise, articulate and entertaining presentation. Earn their attention. When you are able to do that you will notice your attendance growing and earning more time to deliver your message. Remember that you bought the meal. It is your meeting. Control the meeting and the agenda. Know who is in the meeting. Who are the producers? Who are the "centers of influence?" Who is in management? Who is there for the "free lunch?" Who is there to "heckle" you? Play to the office. Know who you trying to influence. Don't let a heckler control your meeting.

Early in my wholesaling career, I was very respectful of everyone in my lunch meetings. I tolerated "hecklers." I answered of the question of the people who were in the room just "for the free" sandwich.

One day, I was in a lunch meeting with 35 advisors. I had been in this office numerous times. I was getting decent production in the office, but felt I should be doing better. I was delivering what I always thought were high quality meetings. I just was not getting the same responses that I normally get in similar offices.

There was a top producer, who did very little with me, who would always sit in the back of the room and ask a "negative" question within two minutes of the start of the meeting. Almost immediately after the question his assistant would peek her head in the door and tell him he had a call. He would take his food and leave. I would try to get the meeting headed back in the right direction. This happened every time I was in the office.

I had done my homework. I wanted to influence this guy. Things were not improving in the office and this advisor was ruining my meetings. Finally I snapped. The next time I was in the office the same thing happened. He asked his negative question. Then his assistant stuck her head in the room. He stood up a picked up his lunch. With that I blurted out, "Ralph, are you coming back?" He looked at me. The room fell silent. I then told him to leave his lunch. If he came back it would still be there. But, if he was not there to learn then he did not earn the right eat the lunch that I bought. With that he threw his sandwich in the trash and stormed out. All I could think was that was not smart. I was probable done in the office. Shortly after the "moment," the silent room broke out in laughter. The advisors in the room told me that he does that in every lunch meeting and that they were embarrassed every time it happened. They thanked me for doing what I did. He never came back to my lunch meeting. The office production went through the roof. And believe it or not, Ralph became a solid producer for me. The office appreciated me taking charge of the meeting room and being a leader by making the difficult decision. I am not telling you to kick the hecklers out of the office, but you need to find a way to control your room and the moment.

Be a leader.

Be Honest
Be Ethical

People do business with people they "know and trust." How true that statement is. The longer you are in the business the more it becomes obvious that many people are not ethical or honest. We live in a world of greed. As wholesalers we are trained to sell more and more. There is tremendous pressure for wholesalers to produce large numbers. The same holds true with our clients. We live in an environment where people will try to find shortcuts or an edge. Over my years I have seen wholesalers that look like heroes. They are revered by their firm because their sales have jumped. They are given all sorts of praise and honors. When your sales jump like that you can usually smell a rat. My experience tells me that it is only a matter of time before that person crashes and burns. When that happens, it is amazing how that person is avoided like the plague. There are no short cuts to success.

I once worked with a young wholesaler in the Mid Atlantic. We were working for a young Mutual Fund Distribution firm. There were about 10 wholesalers in our channel. In his first year with the firm his sales were good. The following year we saw an enormous leap in sales. We had become pretty good friends while we were there. We talked about ideas and strategies. I found it interesting that during his jump in sales he appeared to be doing the same things as he was doing before. I just assumed that he was working harder. The more successful his sales number became, the more vacation time he took. At this point I started to scratch my head. How could his sales be going up so dramatically while working less? I could not figure it out. He was awarded and revered at the National Sales Meeting. The following year he was made a regional sales manager. That turned out to be the beginning of the end for him. They had replaced him in the territory with a good friend of mine. In his first year his sales were down. The sales management was pressuring him. We often talked about what was happening in the territory. Finally it all started to make since. One day, the new wholesaler was called into an advisor's office and wanted to know when he come expect his quarterly check. The wholesaler did not have a clue as to what he was saying. The advisor pulled out a file outlining the quarterly payments made to this advisor for seminar help. The interesting thing about this was that there were never any seminars. It was obvious to him that the old wholesaler was buying business with the firm's money. Immediately after the meeting the new wholesaler called me. This was not the first time we had seen something like this in our business. The problem was how he confronts the old wholesaler, who is now his boss, about the situation. I recommended that before you confront him on the situation that he checks with other advisors. He looked for advisors that had a large jump in sales the previous year and had a recent decline in sales. He went to them and asked what he was not doing that the previous wholesaler was doing. They all said the same thing. The previous wholesaler was sending large seminar support checks. Once he had enough to go on, he went to the National Sales Manager and explained that he was being asked for seminar money. He asked the NSM if he could look back and find out if we had a record of how much seminar support had been given in the territory. The NSM got the run from the finance department. Once he got the run it became obvious what had happened in the territory. It was not long before the "Golden Boy" was no longer with the firm. The new wholesaler was left alone to build the territory the proper way. As of today, the old wholesaler is nowhere to be found and the new wholesaler has had a very successful wholesaling career.

That is obviously a severe case. Whether it is severe or a "little white lie" you cannot fool the clients. Just the other day I was asking an advisor about what turns him off about wholesalers. He said that there is a wholesaler that he likes, but has the habit of cancelling meetings. Over the years this wholesaler has cancelled numerous meetings. Each time he has a different excuse. It had become clear that the excuses usually were not legitimate. He said that he stopped giving him any new business about two years ago. He says that he really likes the guy. He has great meetings and delivers great information, but he cannot trust him anymore. He said that no matter how good his products are or how good his meetings are he cannot do business with someone he cannot trust or count on.

Products, research and funds come and go, but honesty and integrity are yours forever. Honesty cannot and should not be sold. Your word is your bond. You will have many opportunities to take a shortcut or give a dishonest answer to a tough situation because it looks to be the easy way out. Do not be tempted. Once you go down that path you can never turn back. The longer you are in the business you will recognize that most advisors will do business with you in good and bad markets because they do business with people that they "know and trust."

Build an Advisory Council

One of the smartest things a wholesaler can do is build an "Advisory" of clients. Many successful businesses have a board. Sometimes we get so wrapped up in what we're doing that we fail to recognize things. It can benefit a wholesaler to employ other eye, ears and ideas.

Someone once told me the best way to observe your business is to "sit across the street" and observe your business. We live and work with blinders on. While we think that we know everything about our business, there are opportunities and problems that we never see. It is like driving down the road and thinking everything is going fine. Another car pulls up next to you and tells you that one of your tail lights is out. You couldn't see that your tail light was out, but without them you could run into trouble. Without the assistance of the other driver you would have never known you had a problem.

The same thing holds true with wholesaling. There will be times when you are going down the wrong path or you are missing an opportunity. If you have an extra set of eyes, ears and ideas, you can run a more efficient practice.

Select a handful of your best clients from a diverse background. Ask if they would be interested in helping you with your practice and be willing to meet occasionally to discuss how they would help make you a better wholesaler.

Make sure that you meet as a group at least semi-annually. You will learn so much about yourself. At first you will feel inadequate. Then you will feel that they don't understand anything about wholesaling. It is important to understand that what they observe about you and wholesaling is invaluable. Learn to take the information and insight and learn how to use it to better your business. If you are missing a wholesaler tail light they will be there to tell you.

Over the years I found the best way to conduct these meeting was in an informal setting. We would go bowling, play bocce ball, or played golf before dinner. That way everyone had a chance to let their guard down and open up. At dinner we would get down to business and have great conversations about the industry, what was happening at their firms, other wholesalers and my practice.

There were other great results from building an "Advisory" group. Not only did I get some tremendous insight through their eyes, but they felt empowered. They all loved to pick up their phones and tell me what other wholesalers that stopped by were doing or what their firm was about to do that could impact my business. Because they felt a responsibility to my success they increased their production with me and became a great referral network.

Building and "Advisory" may sound like a silly idea, but if you don't there is a good chance that you are driving around with your tail lights out. That is a problem that you could have avoided if you had someone that you could trust to tell you.

Be Yourself

One of the best things you can do to be a top wholesaler is to be yourself. Do not try to be someone you are not. It sounds simple enough, but you would be surprised with how wholesalers get away from who they are and what got them to the position that they currently have. What do I mean by be yourself? If you are professor like, then act professor like. If you have an artistic side, then show that side. If you are focus and organized, then be focused and organized. Here is why. People do business with people they know and trust. Let your clients get to know YOU. If you are honest with yourself and portray the real you then it will be easier for your client to trust you. If they KNOW YOU and TRUST YOU, then you are well on your way to being successful.

I have a very good friend that I wholesaled with years ago. He was and ex-tight end for the University of Florida football team. He was a charismatic, good looking guy that was covering North Florida. This was a "can't miss" combination. He got off to a quick start, but eventually fell off the charts. We often talked on the phone. We spoke mostly about social things. After his calls I would feel good and energized. I simply could not figure out why this guy was struggling. There was not an office this sports stud could not get into. He continued to struggle. At our first national sales meeting it hit me. He was the guy in the audience that was trying to ask all the sophisticated questions of the analyst. I asked the other wholesaler in the state if that was how he acted in the territory. He said that the knock on him was that he was trying to act like an analyst in his meetings. The clients were uncomfortable with him. If he was true to himself and played the part of the University of Florida football player turned wholesaler, he would have cleaned up in the territory. People wanted to talk football and be around this charismatic personality. He was very bright and knew his products well. Unfortunately, he did want to be known as the football player, but wanted people to think of him as the analytic type. His wholesaling career was short-lived.

I was an art major in college. I also play football, hockey and lacrosse in college. Not exactly the pedigree people are looking for in the business. I can promise you this, nobody was better on a grease board than me. I used that "artsy, fartsy" part of my personality to my advantage. My presentations and meetings were more creative than others. That was who I was and that is what the clients liked about me.

If you have a natural skill or advantage, play to it.

Be a Student of Your Craft

What sets great wholesalers apart from good wholesalers is knowledge of their trade. There are so many aspects to wholesaling. It is important to know your products, be a quality presenter, know your competition, know your client, know all the systems and platforms your clients use and the many techniques to be a better sales person.

There is an overwhelming amount of information to digest and things seem to change on a regular basis. If you think you know it all, wait a month and something will change. Your firms do what they can to keep the wholesaler informed and trained, but that is not enough. It is up to the wholesaler to be self trained.

I was a specialist at Merrill Lynch for two years, which meant that I had a chance to see how hundreds of wholesalers practiced their craft. I was amazed with the lack of training and knowledge of the industry. I knew firsthand how difficult and time consuming it was to stay on top of your craft. It was apparent that other wholesalers were not spending the time to master their craft.

Going to National Sales Meeting, Regional Sales Meetings, Training Meetings and Conference Calls is not enough to keep up with the trade. If you want to separate yourself from the competition, go the extra mile because most of your competition is not.

Presentation skills are imperative. It appears that many, if not most; wholesalers are just going through the motions when giving a presentation to an audience. That approach is disastrous. For many advisors, this will be their first contact with you. That goes back to the previous chapter when I reminded you that "you only get one chance to make a first impressions," Many advisors are auditioning you for possible seminar opportunities.

In all my research with advisors they say they can identify a quality wholesaler by the presentations they give. You may not see the importance in giving presentations, but if you want to be a top wholesaler you had better learn to be an outstanding presenter.

Just like you, I have had all the presentation training that your firm has supplied. Have you ever sat in those classes and said to yourself, all these wholesalers are great presenters? My guess is no. It is important to set yourself apart and be the best presenters. Take the time to be the best. Take all your presentation training and practice. Go out and buy a video machine and tape yourself. Keep practicing in front of that video machine until you believe you have an impactful presentation.

Now that you are ready, take that video machine to your meeting. This time set your machine up to film the audience. When you play it back pay close attention to how the audience responds positively and negatively to your presentation. Go back and work on that presentation. Emphases the positive parts and change or eliminate the negative parts. The $250 you spend on the video machine will be worth its weight in gold. It would also be worth hiring a presentation coach or tutor.

When I first started wholesaling I hired a professor from a local university to help me build presentations and find a personal presentation style. I used this professor for years to help build presentations and refine my style. I clearly separated myself from the competition when it came to giving presentations. This catapulted me to the top of the list when top producers were looking at doing seminars. It also opens doors to the hard to reach producers.

The number one thing advisors expect is for you to know your products. As a group we are fairly adept at this. The advisor wants to know that their wholesaler knows about what their firm offers in products, value added knowledge and the firms macro view on the markets. Where you can really make a difference is fitting your products in with the competitions products. There is nothing more impressive than a wholesaler that knows not only their products, but also knows the ins and outs of the competitions products.

When I first got into wholesaling my National Sales Manager suggested getting "Principia" (the Morningstar software comparing all Mutual Funds.). He said that he would sit around at night and the weekends watching television with his family while using "Principia." He said he would compare and contrast his products with the competition. I took his advice and bought "Principia."

When I first started wholesaling we were trying to explain

why our products were better than the competitions. I knew exactly why our product was better than the competitions.

Back then, if you had a better product, you got the "ticket." It was like shooting fish in a barrel. As the advisor got more sophisticated it was not strictly about competing with other funds, but it was about complementing other funds. Then it was all about MPT (modern portfolio theory) statistics. As time goes on and there is more information, data and knowledge the more sophisticated the advisory becomes.

The more that things change, the more they stay the same. Make knowing your competition a passion. When an advisor can get all the product knowledge from one source they will be an invaluable asset to that advisor. That advisor will always find room in their portfolio for your products. Knowledge is gold.

Knowing your client seems so obvious, but it is where most wholesalers fall short. We have been trained in certain questioning sequences over the year, but we do not do enough to use the knowledge we gain from the questioning. In my research, the advisor knows when a wholesaler is questioning them. They are just waiting for that wholesaler to eventually push a product on them based on the answers the advisor gave them. It is obvious that the wholesaler is guiding the advisor down a path. During the questioning sequence the wholesaler uncovers some valuable intelligence but fails to use that information in the future.

Many wholesalers are required to use the questioning sequence by their sales management. I am not saying that is wrong. I am saying that we need to use all that information in the future.

It is so important to take the time after the meeting to log in the knowledge after the meeting. This is one of the areas that I struggled at. I would walk out of a meeting and go into other meetings. By the time my day was done I had a lot of intelligence in my head. I would go home and get busy with my family. The next day I would get up and start the process all over again. I would never write anything down and organize the intelligence. A month later I would visit that advisor again and gather the intelligence again.

I had a good friend in Minnesota that helped me organize the information. He told me that he bought a tiny tape recorder. After each meeting he would slip into a quiet area and review the meeting on his recorder. He carried many little tapes in his briefcase. Each advisor would have a dedicated tape. After he got home he would file that tape. The night before the next meeting he would replay the entire tape (multiple meetings). He would walk into the next meeting well armed with knowledge and a strategy for that meeting. I adopted this method and I was amazed with how well prepared I was for my meetings and how the Advisor appreciated how knowledgeable I was with their practice.

This technique did not take much time. Everybody needs a strategy for documenting their meeting. Knowledge is gold. Don't lose it.

Knowing your clients and prospects systems and platforms is an opportunity in today's marketplace. As a Specialist at Merrill Lynch in recent years, I can tell you that this is more important than you think. The advisor is inundated with enormous amount of systems, products and platforms. Wholesalers just assume that the advisors knows all about what their firm has to offer. They don't.

If you want to separate yourself from your competition, learn these firms systems and platforms.

There was a wholesaler that I worked with in Chicago who concentrated his attention on the advisors retirement business. This wholesaler went out of his way to make sure he knew more about each firm's retirement platforms than anyone else.

When I say "anyone," I am not just talking about the competition. He knew more than the firm's specialist. As a specialist I would take him on my retirement meetings because not only did he know our platform better than I did, but I also used those meetings to learn. Do you think his knowledge of the platform benefited him? You can bet on it. His products were in all the proposals I did for my advisors. His meetings with the largest retirement producers were an education for anyone in the room. The intellectual meeting with the advisor and the wholesaler was extraordinary.

The breadth of knowledge and information being passed between the two parties was enlightening. I can tell you this. The wholesaler was a true partner with these advisors.

Every wholesaler needs to learn about their clients internal systems. Find a client or friend in each firm to guide you through their systems.

Learn how to navigate the system. Learn the language they use when talking about the systems. Play with the system. Find out how you can implement your products, value added materials and research into their systems. Once you feel comfortable navigating the systems you will be an invaluable asset to the advisor.

The advisor is very impressed when a wholesaler can guide them through their system when talking about a money manager's products, value added material and research. If you leave a marketing piece it will be thrown out. If you tell them about your "stuff," they will forget it. If you show them on their system and tag it as a "favorite" they will use it.

Why will they use it? They will use it because it is easy to find and easy to use.

Remember, the advisor is looking to simplify their life, not making it more complicated.

I have a friend in Florida that is a very successful wholesaler. I will never forget when he showed up at a sales meeting. He had a back ground in computers. When we were in a "brain storming" session, he said that he was building his business by setting up clients "contact management" programs. Back then "contact management" software was relatively new. I thought to myself, this guy will be done within a year.

He called me about two months after the meeting. He told me that he was running around installing and training advisors, and their teams, with ACT (a "contact management" software). What did this have to do with selling products? Now I thought that he would not make it through the month.

As time went on I started to see his numbers move up. I thought to myself, he must have seen the light and started pushing product (Product pushing was the selling strategy back then.). When I saw him at the next meeting I asked how things were going? I thought he was going to say that he started to be more product focused. He said that he was scheduled to install and train all the top producers in two wire house firms in his territory.

He said that they paid him by doing his products. I was wrong. This guy used technology to separate him from the other wholesalers.

To this day, if I need knowledge on firms systems and how a wholesaler can use that knowledge I call him. Obviously, systems and sophistication has improved since then, but the strategy still works. If you can learn the firms system and assist them in using their systems to improve their practice then you will become an invaluable member of their team. They will find a way to use your product.

I will never forget my second grade teacher constantly reciting to us, "Good, Better, Best. Never let it rest until your Good is Better and your Better is Best." That is a lesson that we should all take to heart when it comes to mastering our craft. We constantly need to work to get better. Read everything you can. Get as much sales training as you can. As soon as you get comfortable with your level of knowledge, don't stop learning. One of the beautiful things about our business is that it always changes. With change comes opportunity. Never get comfortable. Keep mastering your craft. If you don't, someone else will.

Incorporate Yourself

Even though you carry the bag of a specific firm, you must sell yourself. The firms that we work for supply us with the products, territories, marketing and support. However, at the end of the day it is YOU that sells. You must think of yourself as a franchisee. If you own a McDonald's you are given a territory where you have exclusive rights. They supply you with the food, drinks, marketing and support. McDonald's will supply you with everything you need, but the success of the store is the responsibility of the franchisee. The same is true in wholesaling. We are supplied with everything we need to be successful. At the end of the day, the success of your territory sits squarely on your shoulders.

You should think of yourself as the sole proprietor of "You Incorporated." Once you get your mind wrapped around that idea then you will be headed in the right direction. I can't tell you how many times wholesalers expect their firm to sell for them. The wholesalers want better products. They want better marketing. They want better internal sales support. There is always a reason why they are not having success. They believe that their failures are the fault of the firm.

You must decide what you can control. Can you control your money managers and their performance? Can you control your management and the decisions they make? Can you control your marketing and the literature that they produce? Can you control the internal sales desk and what they do on a day to day basis? The answer to those questions are no.

Now ask yourself, can I control my activity and whom I see? Can I control my relationships and what my advisors think of me? Can I control my integrity and I can deliver on my word? Can I control my attitude? Can I control my professionalism? The answers to those questions are yes.

When you go into a client's office think to yourself, what if they close down my best selling fund? What if my firm downsizes and my territory is eliminated? What if I go to another firm? Will you still have clients that want to do business with you?

Remember, we are a commodity. Every firm has products, marketing and support. Every firm has a wholesaler in your territory. The difference between success and failure in your territory boils down to you. You need to separate yourself from the pack. You need to rise above your competition. Many of the previous chapters helped you understand how you rise above the competition.

When you have come to grips with the reality that your success is in your hands you will make better business decisions. Everything you do will have a long-term effect with your clients and prospects. You must know that the advisors have a long memory. What you do today will come back to roost years down the road.

I will never forget many years ago when I was asked by a big producer for some help with an RFP (request for proposal). This was memorable because this advisor never did any business with me but I knew that he was a center of influence in the office.

It did not take up much of my time to gather the information for him. He was very thankful for my help, but still did not do any business with me. I knew he wouldn't because he only used mutual funds in two asset classes. We did not have any funds in his space.

Shortly after that event my territory got cut and no longer covered that office. A few years passed and I switched firms. Once again I was covering that office.

I went into that office to get reacquainted with some of my old clients and friends. I stopped by to say hello to the gentleman with the RFP. We just chatted about what I had been doing for the past few years. Eventually he asked what funds he should look at. I remembered what asset classes he did (because I had a long contact sales record on him). I told him that I had a product that fit his asset class. Before I could tell him about the fund, he asked me if the fund was any good. I told him it was a nice fund. I told him you will find funds with a better track record, but you won't find many funds with a better downside protection. He said "that is all I need to hear. You will see a couple of million dollars placed in that fund over the next couple of months."

He then looked at me and said "I still owe you for the help you gave me with an RFP from a few years ago. You knew that I did not have an asset class for you, but you still helped me with my proposal and I never forgot that."

The two million dollars and more came over the next few months. That proved to me that clients do business with people not products. The flip side of that is the fact that money came from a wholesaler that had rubbed that advisor the wrong way. The wholesaler had a car with his firm's name on his license plate. He constantly parked his car in the reserved parking spot for guests. He was told not to park there more than once. The fact that he kept parking his car in the reserved spot really irritated this advisor. He was just waiting for a reason to eliminate that wholesaler's products from his book and I was the reason. By the way, there was nothing wrong with the wholesaler's product; there was just a problem with *him*.

Advisors buy products for a reason. It does not happen by accident. They are usually buying a product because of a person. If that was not the case then the top performing fund would get all the business and they would not need us.

You work for yourself. Come to grip with that and what that means and you will be well on your way to a happy and fruitful career.

Take an Interest in Your Client

It is often said, as I have mentioned in earlier chapters, "people do business with people they know and trust." That is easier said than done. It is often difficult for clients to crossover to the "casual side" when they are in their office. Every time you are in a client's office you should find out a little more about your client's outside their office. Most advisors have interest beyond the office. That interest is often right in front of your eyes when you walk in the client's office. If you walk into a client's office and see stuffed ducks hanging on their office wall, there is a better than good chance they are an avid hunter. If you see pictures of their kids wearing youth sports uniforms, there is a good chance that they spend a lot of their time with their kids and their sport teams. If you enter a client's office and there are pictures of them in many different countries, there is a good chance that they enjoy traveling. Find a way to cross over from the business side and find out what is important to them outside the office. People love to talk about their passions. When you get into their outside passions two things will happen. First, you will learn more about what makes them tick. Second, they will think they had a great meeting with you because they spent time talking about themselves and that always makes them feel great. The information you uncover in these meetings may be the most important intel you will ever uncover.

Once you find out what makes your client tick outside the office, take the time to learn more about those interests and how you can crossover into their world. In the case of the advisor with the birds hanging on his office wall, I found out that he was an avid hunter of water birds in Alabama. He spent all his vacation time traveling down to Alabama with friends to hunt. I was not a hunter, but I found a way to get involved in his passion. I would get on the Internet each month and pull up articles about hunting in Alabama. I would read the articles. When I found one that I thought he might find interesting I would send it to him. For a year I would send him these articles. He would always call and thank me for thinking about him. We would talk about the articles and his experiences. He knew that I was not a hunter, but wanted to educate me about his passion. Our meetings always would end in a long conversation about hunting. He would tell me all about his last trip or about his next trip. Eventually, he talked me into going on one of his hunting trips with him. Needless to say, I was thrilled when I got the invitation. I knew that I had crossed over to the "casual side." I took him up on the offer. He taught me how to hunt birds and I met his "best buddies." I still have not become a hunter, but I have become knowledgeable about my client's passion. I went back to Alabama with him on an annual trip for several years. Not only did he become one my best clients, but one of his "buddies" was also an advisor in my territory and became a great client.

The clients with the pictures of their kids in their youth sports uniforms are an easy one for me. If someone were to walk into my office they would find the same types of photos. Once you find out about their children and what and where they play their youth sports, learn more about them. Often the clients that have kids playing "travel" sports are very involved with their kids and their teams. Learn more about their kids and their teams. Because I was very involved with my kids and their teams I had a good idea about their kid's teams. I would always ask about how their kid's teams were doing. I would usually get a long answer to those questions. If the advisor showed a great passion for youth sports I would use that to cross over to the "casual side." I would get their schedule and find out when they would be playing a game close to me. I would find a way to stop by and watch some of their game. They were so thrilled that I would take the time out of my day to watch their kid. They next time I was in their office it was clear that I was much more than a wholesaler. I had become a friend. Trust me on this, that client would tell his colleagues about me stopping by. That put me in great standing with everyone in the office.

I once worked with a wholesaler who covered the panhandle of Florida, Alabama and Georgia. I will never forget sitting in a regional meeting doing product presentations in front of our regional manager and peers. This gentleman got up and did his presentation on our High Yield fund. His presentation was not up to the standard of the regional manager, in the manager's mind. To tell you the truth, it was no better or no worse than most of the other presentations. The manager jumped all over this wholesaler in front of us all. The wholesaler fought back. He told his manager, in his territory, "that is how he does it." He went on to explain that in his territory it is more important to "bird hunt" than present some High Yield presentation. On the surface the wholesaler sounded off base. How could it be more important to "bird hunt" than give high quality presentations? The reality was he made a great point. In his territory a great number of his advisors were avid "bird hunters." In their eyes, if you were not one of them then you were not accepted in their world. This wholesaler spent a great deal of time crossing over into the "casual side." That meant getting involved in the advisors leisure activities. Ten years later many wholesalers have come and gone, but he is still one of the top wholesalers in the territory and still "bird hunting." This wholesaler took an interest in his clients in and out of the office. His advisors became his friends.

You want to cross over to the "casual side." Take the time to learn about what makes your clients tick outside the office. Take an interest in their interests. Don't be phony about it, but show that you are interested in them beyond the office. Remember, "people do business with people they know and trust." They can't get to trust you if they don't know you. It is important to get out of the office and get to know your client and vice versa.

We Sell a Commodity

While we all would like to think that our money managers, funds and research are better than everyone else, the reality is that we're no different than many of our competitors. The reality is that we sell a commodity. We spend countless hours listening to the home office talk about how wonderful their managers are and why they are the best. We also are trained in what sets ourselves apart from the competition. Take the time and ask your advisors about the managers that come through their offices and you find out they think that we are just a commodity. To prove we are a commodity, take a look at the sales in each territory versus the competition. If your products were better than everyone else then each wholesaler would be the top producer in every territory. That however is not the case. Every territory has a different pecking order. Once you understand that we are simply a commodity selling a commodity, you then will set yourselves up for success. The reason why you are on your way to success is because in your mind you are trying to figure out how to separate yourselves from the competition. Ask yourself this question. What separates ME from my competitors?

The best producing wholesalers spend great amounts of time learning how to separate their selves from others. You need to constantly read, listen and learn. Learn what makes other people in our business successful. Who are the top producers in your firm? What makes them special? Who is the top wholesaler in your territory? What makes them special? Talk to the top wholesalers in your firm. The next time you are at a national sales meeting, find time to get with the top wholesalers and pick their brain for ideas. Always ask your advisors who they feel is the best wholesaler and why they feel that way. I always used national and regional sales meetings to gather ideas. As you can tell in this book, I talked to everyone. I wanted to know what everyone way doing. I wanted to know if there was something else I could be doing in my territory. There were times I thought some wholesalers were going down the wrong path. Instead of completely dismissing an idea I would pay close attention to the wholesaler's performance. If I see a significant jump in sales, then the idea is not that crazy. What I have learned over the years is that there is no bad idea.

If you are selling a commodity then you had better keep a close eye on your competition. When you are comfortable in what you are doing in the territory, this is when you are vulnerable. There are always other wholesalers that are trying new things to separate themselves from others. Again, some of the ideas might sound crazy. If it turns out that it is not a crazy idea, then you will need to combat that wholesaler in order not to lose clients. Do not fall asleep at the wheel. Keep pushing the envelope.

The other place to learn is from successful people and businesses outside of our industry. Learn what other successful sales companies are doing and see if there is a way to use their strategies in your practice. As I have mentioned before, I spent a lot of time and effort to become a top presenter in the industry. I hired a tutor to help build presentations. We built well thought out and informative presentations. They were organized and effective presentation. One day I called my tutor and said that I needed my presentations to be more entertaining and memorable. What could I do to take my presentations to the next level? My tutor told me that because of television shows like Sports Center and MTV people's attention spans were changing. People were not as interested in the traditional news telecasts anymore. They were drawn to quick sound bites like they get on ESPN and MTV. We learned from that and started building presentations with sound bites. Instead of presentation with a smooth flowing, well organized and informative approach, I was presenting multiple sound bites in an informative, entertaining format. I quickly found that there was more energy in the meeting room and my attendance started to grow. That change in style caused a large increase in my production.

It is so important not to be in the crowd, but to be ahead of the crowd. Never stop learning and pushing the envelope. Remember, we are selling a commodity. What makes you different? As one of my past managers would say; "get ahead of the wave."

Conclusion

We all work in a very complicated business. Where else can you find a major job in a major industry where the lines of selling, marketing, servicing and prospecting are so blurred? Think about other major industries. Most, if not all other industries, have very defined processes to sell. They are trained to do it the same way. You sell their way or you don't sell for them. These firms have a very robust and extensive training.

It is mind boggling that such a major industry with highly compensated sales people has virtually no formal sales training. For all the sophistication and specialty of the wholesaling business it was only a matter of time until that lack of training began to lessen the quality of the wholesaling.

The reason for writing this book was to help wholesalers become better at their trade. After reading this book you are probably saying to yourself "how can anyone do everything" that is written? The reality is you probably can't.

The beauty of our business is that you can never perfect all aspects of wholesaling. There is always room to improve. Only one wholesaler can be the best. Everyone else is chasing. If that "best" wholesaler does not continue to get better it won't be long until another wholesaler passed them by.

My second grade teacher used to put a saying up on the blackboard every day and it still rings true today for our business. It goes like this. "Good, better, best. Never let it rest, until your good is better and your better is best."

It was with this in mind that I started my business, Good | Better | Best Inc., and wrote this book. I believe that we needed someone who carried the bag successfully, that would go into the "field" and train and coach other wholesalers.

In this book I have a chapter on building a "plan" or a "blueprint." In that chapter I mention that you should have a plan to improve your skills and knowledge. This book is designed to help all wholesalers, regardless of your experience and production level. This book will give you some new ideas on how to improve your business. I designed the book to be an easy read and make you think about how you can improve.

I also have a section with 101 Pointers. Tear out these pages or copy them down on a separate sheet of paper. Stick those "pointers" in your bag and occasionally review them. It should motivate you to continue to follow through with the things that you are doing correctly and reminds you where you need improvement.

If you are very serious about being the best you can be make the investment in your practice and hire me to travel in the field and "coach" you on your skills. You can contact me at mike@ gotcoach.net.

Thank you for reading this book and investing in making yourself the best you can be. Remember what my teacher beat into me. "Good, better, best. Never let it rest, until your good is better and your better is best."

101 Pointers

Pointer 1   It's a numbers game.

The more people you see, the better your results will be. Regardless of the routing system or coverage system you practice, maximize the number of people you see.

Pointer 2   Under promise and over deliver.

So often I run into people that promise me the "world" and fail to deliver on the promise. It is important to control expectations. Never promise more than you can deliver. A good strategy would be to under promise what you can deliver. There is nothing more impressive than when someone gives you more than you expect. Everyone loves a bonus.

Pointer 3   Build a marketing library.

Over the years you will come upon many marketing pieces and ideas that have worked for you. You also run into other peoples and firms marketing pieces that work. Gather any and all good pieces and start a marketing library. You will be amazed how you will use those pieces or develop similar pieces years down the road.

Pointer 4   Play to your strengths.

Find out where your strengths are and use them to the fullest.

Most people have strength in either presenting, question sequencing, relationship building, analytics, etc. Identify that strength and play to it. If you have a skill that you excel at then it would benefit you to play to your strength.

Pointer 5   Be able to cut the cord.

One of the hardest things to do is to walk away from an opportunity. You will run into customers that want too much from you. They may want too much time, support, assistance or price. Even though it is not natural to want to walk away from business, it is important to recognize when a relationship is negatively impacting your business. Sometimes you need to prune a blossom to get more blossoms.

Pointer 6   Build an idea bank.

Any time you have a marketing idea or thought, jot down your thought and file it away. Also collect ideas you hear from your clients and colleagues. Review all these ideas on a regular basis. You will find a good idea today will be a great idea down the road. You should never have a shortage of ideas. Ideas are the life blood of your creativity.

Pointer 7   Work smarter.

Have a plan. Don't just react. Be smart about how you go about your business. Before you schedule, prospect, market, meet with an advisor, etc. plan how you are going to approach the situation. This will make you more efficient and effective.

Pointer 8   Compartmentalize your conversations.

Whether you are having a personal or business conversation, it is important to keep those conversations to yourself. If you tell others of your conversation it will eventually get back to your client. This will demonstrate distrust. That is not a reputation you want. Leave your conversations in the right compartment.

Pointer 9   Smile and dial.

When on the phone with your clients and prospects remember to smile. It may sound strange, but if you are smiling when you are on the phone it comes across on the other end. It may seem like a small thing but your enthusiasm will come through the phone and can be the difference between a successful call and a failed call.

Pointer 10   Divide your Clients/Prospects into groups.

Scrub your client list. Separate your clients/prospects into definable groups of advisors that have something in common. Identify the group in which you have a common bond or interest with. If this is a group you have success with or enjoy covering you will be more motivated to cover them and similar advisors. By doing this you will be able be more effective in covering or prospecting them.

Pointer 11   Be truthful.

Sometimes the easiest way to get from "Point A" to "Point B" is to stretch the truth. While most of what you are delivering to the client is the truth, it is the stretching of that truth that will cause skepticism with the client. Skepticism is another word for distrust. Remember that clients do business with people they know and trust. A "little white lie" will kill the trust.

Pointer 12   Use multiple colors.

When presenting on grease board be sure to use colors. Colors can bring a presentation to life. Colors are very emotional and emphasis key parts of your presentation. A black and white board can be dull. A colorful board will capture the audience attention.

Pointer 13   Divide your clients geographically.

After you have separated your clients into segments, separate them into geographic segments. You want to break your territory into smaller, more efficient sub-territories. You will be able to see more people and typically it is easier to get advisors to play off other advisors and get referrals in smaller territories. In smaller territories it is more likely that advisors know and interact with one another.

Pointer 14   Your word is your bond.

So often you have heard the saying "say what you mean and mean what you say." If you live by that credo then you are well on your way to demonstrating trust. If your customers know that you stand behind what you say then they will view you as reliable.

Pointer 15   Create a presentation sticker.

Develop a sticker that you can place on a grease board or on other presentation boards. Get the stickers that will peel right off without causing any damage. The sticker should have your firms name and logo, your name, your number and your email address. Not only will it bring professionalism and life to your presentation, but you will find that many advisors will stick them on the walls after you leave. It is nice to know that my name and firm are displayed while other wholesalers are presenting.

Pointer 16   Ask for help.

You'll find that asking your clients how you can grow your business can benefit your practice. It is nice to hear from your clients about where opportunities exist. We are so focused in what we are doing that sometimes we can't see what is right in front of us. It is important to have multiple eyes and ideas.

Pointer 17   Be creative with your clients/prospects.

Sometimes your traditional approach with your clients and prospects will start to lose its effectiveness. It is important to add creativity to your approach. It is important to constantly freshen up your approach. If you get a reputation of having fresh and creative ideas the word will get around and open additional doors to your business.

Pointer 18   Avoid dull presentations.

Work on your presentations. Most advisors find wholesaler presentations to be dull and bland. Add some fun and entertainment to your presentations. Use pictures, sounds and sound bites to spice up a presentation. Bring your presentation to life. It is not just what you say, but how you say it. An effective presentation is like an effective commercial.

Pointer 19   Learn from your peers.

We simply can't know it all. Take the time to learn what other successful colleagues and competitors are doing. It is important to implement other successful strategies into your practice. Sometimes it is important to borrow ideas. If your colleague is having success with a new strategy, there is a good chance you will also. If your competitor is having success with a new strategy it is important to counteract them. Take the time to see what is going on around you.

Pointer 20   Always add to your prospecting list.

You can never have too many prospects. As your business becomes more and more successful it is easy to rest on your laurels. Your lifeline to growth will always be your prospects. The more prospects you have, the greater the chances there are some diamonds in that prospecting list. You must always be asking for names and referrals. You must always be filling the pipeline.

Pointer 21   Don't hand out materials before the meeting.

If you hand out materials before your presentation the audience will be viewing the pieces while you are speaking. If you need a piece to make a point, pass it out while you are making that point. It is important that their focus be on you and not on your marketing piece.

Pointer 22   Learn from others.

Most of your best ideas will come from other successful people and industries. Spend the time to read and learn about how other successful sales businesses run their business. Find if there is a way to adapt their ideas into your business. The advisors are always interested in a new and fresh idea.

Pointer 23   Ask your clients how they want to be covered.

It is important to ask your customers/clients how they want to be serviced. Where and when do they want to meet? How do they want you to deliver information? Be sure that you know the names of their support staff and how you should interact with them. If you fit into their system then you will be more efficient and they will respect you for understanding their business.

Pointer 24   Prepare the room.

Get to your presentation room early. Make sure the room is set up the way you want it. Place the presentation board where the audience can see it and you can write on it without turning your back to the crowd. Make sure the room is clean. Tidy up the room from the previous users. A cluttered room will distract. A neat and organized room will add professionalism to the presentation. Set up the tables and chairs to your liking. A prepared presenter translates to a prepared professional.

Pointer 25   Find your niche and own it.

Find a niche in the market and dominate it. Learn more about a particular niche than your competitors and customers. If you are viewed as the foremost authority in a particular niche then clients, prospects and others will come to you for solutions.

Pointer 26   Don't "just leave materials."

So often wholesalers walk into a situation where the advisor tells the wholesaler to leave material and they will review it. The reality is they probably will not. If you run into that situation it would be more beneficial if you ask them when they have time to meet about what you want to convey to them. You are looking for quality time, not to be brushed aside.

Pointer 27   Know the support staff.

Take the time to learn the names of the advisors and office support staff. These people can become your eyes and ears to the office. They can open a door that may normally be closed. Wholesalers generally ignore these folks. Bring them some of your "trash and trinkets." If you take an interest in them they can be an enormous help to you.

Pointer 28   Maximize your support.

Periodically go back and review who you have financially supported. Identify who you helped with seminars, marketing, support or prospecting. Have they lived up to their end of the partnership? If they have then, find a way support them again. If they have not, then remind them that they need to live up to their end of the deal. You need to get the greatest bang for your buck.

Pointer 29   Listening is your greatest skill.

We are sales people selling to sales people. We often spend a meeting outdueling the advisor at who can speak more. Don't turn the meeting into a competition. Be the listener. Once an advisor gets speaking the most important thing you can do is to listen. They will give you many nuggets of information you will be able to use. They will also feel great about themselves and the meeting.

Pointer 30   Attitude is everything.

Your attitude is your gateway to who you are. It is important to always have a positive and enthusiastic attitude. People want to be around positive people. Don't get dragged into a negative conversation. Stay positive and you will have a positive and fruitful meeting. Be negative and you will have a negative and disappointing meeting.

Pointer 31   Team up with outsiders.

Bring in noncompeting partners that can help your business. Find a way you can implement attorneys, accountants, etc. into your business. They can help build credibility to a meeting or seminar. You want your clients to view your business as a well rounded practice, not just a product provider.

Pointer 32   Develop an "elevator pitch."

People will often ask you what you do? It is important to describe what you can do for them. Develop a 30 second commercial describing what you can do for them. Speak their language and don't use industry jargon. Use this opportunity to paint a picture of what you can do for them. Use words like maximize, proven, develop and increase when describing your services. Remember, what can you do for them?

Pointer 33   Be careful of what you drive and where you park.

Be aware of what car you drive. Clients do pay attention to what you drive. The advisor does not want to see you driving to their office in a car that costs more than many houses. If the name of the car is hard to pronounce by the average person, leave it at home. You don't want to look like you don't need the business. If you cover advisors that work with unions make sure you drive American. Avoid parking in the reserved or visitors parking spots. Those spots are reserved for the Advisor's clients.

Pointer 34   Find a wealth of information library.

Spend time in bookstores, libraries and on online learning from others. Find the time to learn what other successful people are doing. If you have some spare time in your day fill it up with knowledge. Five minutes in a bookstore can earn you the best idea of the year.

Pointer 35   Write hand written "Thank You" notes.

Our business world is getting more impersonal every day. Take the time to write a quick "thank you" note after an advisor meeting. A hand written note is an extremely personal gesture. Order some thank you notes and take one minute to thank the advisor for meeting with you. That will be the best minute you spend in a day.

Pointer 36   Always confirm your appointments.

Make it a habit to always confirm your appointments. This will make you appear organized. It will also make you more efficient with your time. Nothing wastes time like getting to an appointment only to find out that the advisor had to cancel or did not have the appointment on their schedule.

Pointer 37   Subscribe to your clients.

Make sure you subscribe to what your clients subscribe to. Subscribe to the industry magazine that your clients or niche markets are subscribing to. Get the monthly research from the clients that you are covering. Get the asset allocation strategy from the firms that you cover. Know everything they know.

Pointer 38   Build a "Hit List".

Build a list of names of "elephants" that you want to meet. This is a list of advisors who are difficult to meet. Create a plan on how you can get in front of these people. Be creative and aggressive in your pursuit of these advisors. Constantly work to add names to that list.

Pointer 39   Be prepared for each meeting.

Always preview your meeting before entering the advisor's office.

Review your past meetings with that advisor. Have a purpose for the meeting. Have all back up materials readily available. Know the names of their support staff. Get yourself in a positive frame of mind and project confidence and enthusiasm. Remind yourself that you need a referral.

Pointer 40   Build a niche lead list.

Always acquire names of advisors and resources of your niche market. At every meeting ask for names of advisors in the niche market that you specialize in. Always be growing your niche prospecting list. These people will be your future. Also get the names of other noncompeting people in your niche. You may be able to team up with these people to broaden and enhance your practice.

Pointer 41   Build an "Advisory."

Create a focus group of clients that can help you build your business. It is important for you to see your business through your client's eyes. Other businesses use focus groups to learn about marketing, selling and servicing. Your "Advisory" group should do the same. The more eyes and ideas you have the greater chances you have to avoid mistakes.

Pointer 42   Send special notes or cards.

During all your conversations you should find out about special dates such as birthday, anniversaries, etc. It is a nice idea to send a card to your clients on a special day. Other wholesalers will also send cards on the big days such as birthdays and Christmas. I always found out when they passed the series 7 or received their producer number. I would send them an anniversary card congratulating them on another successful year and wish them luck for the next year.

Pointer 43   Know the local concerns.

Know what is going on locally. Know what is happening within a firm and/or branch. Be aware of what is happening in the local news. Be cognoscente of what is on the advisors mind. If you are well versed in the local news then you will better know your customer.

Pointer 44   It's not all about you.

Don't be one of those salespeople that put themselves in front of their clients. Try to avoid the word "I" in your meetings. "I" will make the advisor think that the meeting is all about you. Whenever you can, use the words "we" and "you". "We" sounds like you are looking for a partnership with the advisor. "You" sounds like you care about the advisor and their practice.

Pointer 45   Send links and articles of interest to your clients.

Know your clients and their interests. Take time to surf the internet and read articles on subject matters that interest your clients. Send a link or an article that you believe the client would be interested in. Your client will appreciate that you are thinking about them. This will help cross you over to the "friend" side of your relationship. Make sure that what you are sending is compliant.

Pointer 46   Know the specialist.

The specialist in your territory is a wealth of information. Some specialists have more influence over the advisors than others. Regardless of their influence they are all a wealth of information. They know what the firm's initiatives are currently and in the future. They have abundant intelligence on your advisors and prospects. The specialist should be an invaluable asset for your practice.

Pointer 47 Don't get discouraged, they'll come around.

Don't get discouraged if you don't get the immediate reaction you are looking for when you have an initial meeting with an advisor. Some people take a while to warm up to a new face. These prospects may be skeptical of wholesalers based on something that may have happened in the past. It may take some longer to get to "know you and trust you."

Pointer 48 Cross over to the "friend" side.

At each meeting with an advisor, try to learn more about their interests outside the office. It is important to move a relationship from strictly business to a relationship between friends. People like to do business with their friends. They are also less likely to end a business relationship with a friend.

Pointer 49 Read everything you can about the markets.

Most people read the basics like *Barron's* and the *Wall Street Journal.* Dig deeper. Read as much third party information as you can. For example; find out what the professors at the University of Chicago, N.Y.U., Harvard, Wharton, UCLA, etc. are writing. Read the many independent newsletters. The more broad based your knowledge is the more of a resource you can be for your clients.

Pointer 50 Be a ray of sunlight.

Sales people and advisors often take it all too seriously. Loosen up and have a little fun. While it is important to take care of business, it is also important to put a smile on the advisors face. You don't always need to be selling. Many times you may be the only ray of sunshine in their day. Selling is serious enough, have some fun.

Pointer 51   What do your clients want from you?

Find out what your clients want from you. You also need to know how often they want the information. Make sure you develop a delivery system for that information. Check to make sure the (correct) information was sent. Clients will respect an efficient wholesaler.

Pointer 52   Offer a benefit to your Clients/Prospects.

In today's marketplace advisors are not just buying yield, price or performance. They are buying a solution. Think about what your solution is and how that benefits the client. In this "what's in it for me" society we currently live in make sure that you know what your benefit is to the client.

Pointer 53   Let the advisor know that know them.

It is important for the advisor to know that you know about them, their business and their goals. You need to prove to the advisor that you understand them. Most prospects feel that you don't and won't understand their business. Prove to them that you understand their practice and how you can help them achieve their goals.

Pointer 54   Thank the Advisor for the business.

Be sure to thank your clients for their business. Don't leave it entirely up to your internal. Decide who you need to thank. May I suggest that you call on large purchases or first time buyers? Also be sure that you acknowledge purchases when you are next in their office. Thank them for the business that they did on a specific date. Clients like to know that you saw the transaction and appreciate the recognition.

Pointer 55   Qualify your prospects.

Before you spend time with a prospect do some qualifying. Find out if the prospect has the resources to do significant business with you. Make sure that you have the products and services that they need. You want to spend time on prospects that can become clients not prospects that suck your time dry.

Pointer 56   Dress for success.

Make sure that you dress appropriately for the situation. Wholesaling is no place to make a fashion statement. Wear similar clothing that the advisors are wearing. I have seen too many wholesalers cross the acceptable clothing line. Yes, they do separate themselves from the others. Most of the time that is not the island you want to be on.

Pointer 57   Be responsive to requests.

Every client deserves that you respond to a phone call or email. Not only do they deserve a response, but they deserve an immediate response. Advisors appreciate a responsive wholesaler. Take this opportunity to demonstrate your responsiveness. A response will create a feeling in confidence in you.

Pointer 58   Bring your internal into all conversations.

Make sure that you include your internal in all meaningful conversations with a client/prospect. You spend most of your time in meeting with clients and prospects and will not be able to assist them in a timely manner. The heavy lifting portion of the servicing will be done by your internal. If the internal is aware of the client/prospects needs then they will not have to reinvent the wheel. A strong relationship between the client/prospect and the internal is invaluable.

Pointer 59 Don't leave a lead hanging.

You often run into advisors that tell you to "give them a call." While the comment may have been made in passing it is important to follow up each and every lead. If an advisor gives you a lead on another advisor make sure you follow up that lead immediately. It is important to have a reputation as one that follows up and follows through.

Pointer 60 Do onto others.

You have always heard the saying, "do onto others as you wish them to do on to you." That rings true with wholesalers. Treat all advisors, support people, managers and others as you wish them to treat you. The day may come when you will need their help. They we remember how you had treated them earlier.

Pointer 61 Have an affinity or connection with the niche you choose.

It is important to enjoy what you do. When choosing a niche market or niche clientele, be sure that it is something that interests you. It is much easier to spend time doing research with a subject matter you have an affinity for or visiting with clients that you enjoy interacting with on a daily basis.

Pointer 62 Be honest with your intentions.

If you are trying to earn a prospect's business it is important to be true to your intentions. Let the prospect know your intentions.

Make it clear that you enjoy working in their niche and you enjoy what you do. Tell them what your intensions are and what you will do to earn their business. If you don't, they will think you are just there to use them.

Pointer 63   Pay attention to detail.

In today's marketplace there are many people covering the same people we are. It can be the little things that make you different. Do not overlook the details when covering a prospect or client. Little details could be spending an extra minute to give additional detail to a request or bringing coffee to their assistant. The details can be a huge difference in your coverage versus your competitors.

Pointer 64   Keep everything in perspective

Most days you will run into a difficult situation or set back. Not everything goes as planned. It is important to compartmentalize these issues. Stay positively and focus on the long term plan. Don't let short term setbacks get in the way of your long term success.

Pointer 65   Don't just donate money, donate your time.

You will often be asked by your large clients and prospects to donate money to their charity. While it is important to stay in compliance it also opens a door of opportunity. Learn more about the charity. If it's something you truly are interested in, donate your time also. If your clients/prospects think you care about the same things they care about then they will see you in a different light.

Pointer 66   Be the solution, not the problem.

Be the person that encounters a problem and finds a solution.

On a daily basis we see and hear problems that are internal and external. Instead of being part of the problem or passing it onto someone else, be the person that spearheads a solution. If you have a problem, find a solution. Advisors respect a wholesaler that takes a challenge and delivers a solution.

Pointer 67   Remain thankful.

As you become successful it is important to stay thankful for what got you there. Your success is not an entitlement. Avoid feeling that advisors owe it to you to see you or they owe you something. One of the best ways to destroy a relationship is to convey the attitude of entitlement.

Pointer 68   Be selective with your budget.

Be selective with where you spend your budget money. So often advisors ask for support and the wholesaler just forks it over. Know who you want to spend your budget on and then decide how you can maximize your "bang for the buck." Be proactive with your budget and not reactive.

Pointer 69   Duplicate your top advisors.

Separate your top Advisors into a group. Find out which of those advisors share similarities. Once you have built a sub set of similar advisors, develop a plan to duplicate those advisors. Use those clients for referrals of people like them. Build a plan that targets those prospects and duplicate your best clients.

Pointer 70   Consider the consequences of your actions.

We must make multiple short term decisions every day. Before you react to a short term situation think about the long term affect of your decision. Always think about the consequences of your decisions. That will help you take the appropriate actions.

Pointer 71   Bring a gift to all your meetings.

Advisors seem to love "trash and trinkets." Always try to leave a little reminder of your meeting. Think about using an inexpensive logo pen in you meetings. Use the pen to highlight a point on a research or marketing piece. Then offer the pen to them. When using a grease board at a lunch meeting use some logo markers. After the meeting leave the markers behind. It will cost you pennies, but the impact is priceless.

Pointer 72   Create a routing system.

One of the traps we fall into is to allow our clients to run our schedule. It is important to break your territory into a manageable number of geographic routes. Build your schedule to know when you are going to be in a route for a year out. This way you can run your own schedule. Your clients will get used to knowing how often, and when, you will be in their office. Take control of your schedule and your practice.

Pointer 73   Be positive about yourself.

Avoid talking negatively about yourself. Be careful not to talk about how the markets are negatively impacting you. Don't talk about how a firm's or person's decision will have a negative impact on your business. It is important to stay positive. Your clients don't want to hear about your problems. It is important to turn a negative into a positive. Learn how to "turn chicken poop into chicken salad."

Pointer 74   Find the "Centers of Influence."

It is important to identify the "centers of influence" in a branch, region and firm. Ask your clients and prospects which peers they respect and get ideas from. Once you identify these people, build a strategy to meet these people. These "centers of influence" can help your business in many ways.

Pointer 75   Schedule in advance.

Make sure you schedule important client and prospecting meetings well in advance. Make sure that you schedule office and lunch meetings well in advance. Most branches will allow you to schedule out lunch and office meetings for an entire calendar year. If you want to see the top offices and top advisors you need to get in the front of the line. If you wait to schedule on a Friday for the following week then you will not see the quality advisors you need to see to be a top wholesaler.

Pointer 76   Control your emotions.

I can promise you that things will go wrong. When things do go wrong it is important to keep your emotions in check. You need to shake off any negative thoughts. Remember, every time you interact will clients you are on stage. Your short-term attitude will have a long-term effect.

Pointer 77   Position yourself with a "center of influence."

Before you meet with a "center of influence" individual, make sure you do your research. Find out how you can help their practice. If they view you as a valuable resource they will spread your name to others. Ask for their advice on how they you should connect with others. Make sure you emphasis how you can benefit them rather than just using them for personal gain.

Pointer 78   Fill the pipeline.

Don't let your sales get stagnant. You must always be prospecting. By the time you see a prospect and the time when they start doing steady business it is approximately nine months. If you stop prospecting for three month you find a three month stagnation of sales. Remember to prospect, prospect, prospect.

Pointer 79   Always keep an open mind.

It is important to be aware of everything going on around you. Opportunities are abound. Too often I have seen wholesalers that are closed minded to a new idea. If you are closed minded you may miss an opportunity and prevent self growth.

Pointer 80   Start your day with breakfast.

When prospecting, sometimes it is more effective to meet them for breakfast. Breakfast is a comfortable way to meet with prospects. It allows you to meet before their day gets hectic. Dinner is a bigger investment of their time and is considered more social. Often the prospect does not feel comfortable meeting for dinner on the first meeting. Start with breakfast until they get to know you. A breakfast meeting is a great way to start your day.

Pointer 81   Dump the "time suckers."

You need to lose the advisors that take up more of your time than they are producing for you. Sometimes these are friends. This may make it difficult to cut them lose. If your time is better spent covering prospect and other clients then you need to cut the cord.

Pointer 82   Surround yourself with successful people.

Success can be infectious. In work and life you should surround yourself with other successful people. Successful people are generally positive and are always looking for self improvement. The people you hang out with will have a large impact on whom you are down the road. If you hang with positive and successful people then the chances are that you will be positive and successful. If you surround yourself with negative and unsuccessful people then there is a good chance that you will also fail.

Pointer 83   Be positive when meeting with "centers of influence."

Your attitude will be conveyed to many people. Think about how you want people to think about you. Do you want an influential person to convey to others that you are positive and enthusiastic or negative and presumptuous? Obviously you want to demonstrate that you are a bright, enthusiastic, trustworthy person that can help their business.

Pointer 84   Have a plan.

Call it a business plan, a game plan or a blueprint. What is important is that you have a plan and direction. Build a living document that you can review on a daily basis to make sure that you continue to travel in the right direction. This plan should remind you that you need to prospect, service, educate, etc. Without a plan you will find yourself spinning your wheels.

Pointer 85   Listen or read motivational materials.

This sounds insane, but it is important to listen to motivational tapes and read motivational articles. Listen or read motivational material as often as you can. It can be exhausting trying to "pump" yourself up every day. Use these outside motivational pieces to help "pump" yourself up. This will provide you with the positive energy that you need.

Pointer 86   Be sensitive of the advisor's time.

Time is perhaps the advisor's most precious commodity. It is important to respect the advisor's time. Start by being a few minutes early for your appointment. State how much time you will be taking from their day. Do not overstay your welcome unless they invite you to stay. It is best to finish early. They will appreciate the gift of time and be willing to invite you back.

Pointer 87   Be creative.

There are so many wholesalers that are selling a similar commodity. They have great marketing, research, value added and products. Use your creativity to differentiate yourself from the others. Learn what other successful industries are doing to separate themselves from their competition. Learn what other successful wholesalers are doing to differentiate themselves. There are a ton of great ideas out there. Think outside the box and be creative.

Pointer 88   Things are good when the competition is trashing you.

In our industry there is still a lot of "negative" selling being done by our competition. Be flattered when this occurs. The only reason others are speaking negative of you or your firm is because either they are frightened of you, or want what you have. Clients and prospects see through this archaic tactic. The more people sell negatively against you the more it reiterates to your clients and prospects that you are the competition that they fear. Make sure you don't negative sell. You are only confirming the strength of your competition.

Pointer 89   Stay in touch with the "center of influence."

Make sure that you stay in touch with a "center of influence." So often wholesalers make the initial contact with the "center of influence" and never return. They may not do business with you, but they are influencing many of your clients and prospects. It is important to have an ongoing relationship and not be a one hit wonder. Nobody respects a one hit wonder.

Pointer 90   Set goals.

We all need goals to be successful. Determine what your goals are going to be. Have a long term goal and short term goals. Have product goals, prospecting goals, servicing goal, etc. Reward yourself for accomplishing your goals. Give yourself a reason to go that extra yard to accomplish your goals. Extraordinary wholesalers have extraordinary goals and focus on achieving them.

Pointer 91   Don't judge the book by the cover.

Many of your prospects and clients will have their faults. Do not get stuck on their faults. Look past their warts and find their needs. If you can get past the negative and find their needs then you will have a chance to help them. If you can provide a solution to their needs then you will have a grateful customer and the book cover will look a whole lot better.

Pointer 92   Ask for the referral.

It is always important to ask your customers and prospects for referrals. If your clients appreciate what you bring to their business they will repay you with the gift of a referral. Make sure you articulate what type of referrals you are looking for. Your clients, prospects and "centers of influence" will take great joy in helping you.

Pointer 93   Take control of your office meetings.

Have a plan when you perform an office meeting. Build a creative and informative presentation. When delivering your presentation stay the course. Advisors will try to get you off on a tangent for selfish or innocent reasons. It is important to control the meeting. You paid for the meal. You own their attention. It is your room. Take control of the meeting. Respect their time with a high quality meeting and they will keep coming back.

Pointer 94   Be respectful of others.

Regardless of who the person is, they should be treated with respect. Beside the fact that it is the right thing to do it also could have a long term effect. With all the promotions and demotions that happen in our industry there is a good chance that a subordinate will be elevated to a decision making position. When making a decision the decision maker will remember how you treated them when they were your subordinate.

Pointer 95   Create a referral pitch.

Develop a 30 second pitch on why you need referrals. Explain what type of referrals you are looking to gather. If you have one well organized and brief pitch it will be easier and more comfortable to ask for the referral. It will also remind them that you are similar to them and understand the importance of referrals.

Pointer 96   Learn, Learn, Learn.

Don't rest on your laurels. Every day there is another wholesaler trying to steal your clients. It is important to keep improving your knowledge and skills. Read as much as you can. Take classes to improve your skills. Work with a tutor or business coach. Once you think you know it all, those wholesalers that continue to improve their skills and knowledge will take your clients.

Pointer 97   Be Yourself.

It is so important to be genuine. The client and prospect will see through a counterfeit. It is important to portray the true you to the customers. Remember, people do business with people they know and trust. Let the customer get to know you.

Pointer 98   Update the Advisor on their referral.

Be sure to report back to the advisor on the progress you are making with their referral. They will feel involved and could feel comfortable enough to continue to refer people to you. Advisors hate to give a referral only to find out that the wholesaler never followed up on that lead. Following through is a trait advisors are looking for in a wholesaler.

Pointer 99   Be entrepreneurial.

The best wholesalers are entrepreneurs. They respect that they are given a territory, product, marketing and support. They understand that the rest is up to them. They have the mindset that how much they sell and make is up to them. Take ownership in your territory and run it likes is your own business. If you take ownership in your business you will go that extra mile to succeed.

Pointer 100   Respect your customer's schedule.

Nothing turns off clients and prospects like being late. It is imperative to be prompt. If customers cannot trust you to be on time then will they trust you to deliver solutions? May I suggest taking promptness to a new level? If you schedule a meeting at noon, then arrive at 11:55am. Promptness translates to trustworthiness. Being "fashionably late" is not an attractive quality in this business.

Pointer 101   Thank the Advisor for a referral.

It is important to thank an advisor for every referral they give you. You should always send them a handwritten thank you note. If they are a good referral source or one of their referrals develops into a top client, it would warrant some of your budget money for an appreciation gift.

About the Author

Michael Balch is the President of Good |Better| Best Inc. Prior to starting his own training, consulting and sales organization, he spent twenty-five years in the distribution business with firms such as Kemper, Fidelity, Bank of America and Janus. He held positions from internal wholesaler to National Sales Manager. He always found his way back to his love of wholesaling.

While wholesaling, he was always a top producer. He received multiple awards as "top producer" wherever he went. He worked in start-up territories, middle sized territories and large territories. He also covered all channels and covered every state except Alaska. Regardless of the situation, he always grew his sales at a greater pace than his peers.

Michael is a graduate of Lake Forest College in Lake Forest, Illinois. He currently lives in Wilmette, Illinois with his wife Helen and his four sons.